# INTRO TO
# (*MESSY*) CARE
# AND DISCIPLESHIP

# Intro to ^*Messy* Care and Discipleship

*A Companion Guide*

SCOTT MEHL
RACHEL CAIN
ANN MAREE GOUDZWAARD

Intro to (Messy) Care and Discipleship

© 2020 Scott Mehl, Rachel Cain, Ann Maree Goudzwaard

Additional Contributors: Nate Brooks, Christine Chappell,
Fawn Kemble, Shannon McCoy, Anna Mondal, and Cindy Stashenko

ISBN: 978-1-63342-213-1

**Shepherd Press**
P.O. Box 24
Wapwallopen, PA 18660

www.shepherdpress.com

Scripture quotations are from the ESV® Bible (The Holy Bible, English
Standard Version®), copyright © 2001 by Crossway, a publishing
ministry of Good News Publishers. Used by permission.

*DISCLAIMER*

Names, dates, participants, circumstances, and details have been
rearranged and/or changed in order to protect the people associated
with our stories. Where similarities occurred, permission to share has
been granted. To the best of our ability, we have sought to honor the
privacy and dignity of the participants as well as the good character and
credibility of our authors. The integrity of our ministry to people in
crisis is of utmost concern to our contributors. Any resemblance in these
stories to other persons and/or events should be considered coincidental.

COUNSEL FOR THE HEART
A RESOURCE for WORD-BASED TRANSFORMATION and PRACTICAL DISCIPLESHIP

Cover design by Jacy Corral
Typography by **documen**. www.documen.co.uk
Printed in the USA

# CONTENTS

# INTRODUCTION

Welcome to the *Intro to (Messy) Care and Discipleship*! This material is based on the book, *Loving Messy People*, by Scott Mehl. In this eight-session course, you will learn how to minister to and care for others in the mess of life. This is an opportunity for you to grow in your understanding of the purpose of relationships as they exist in a sinful and fallen world. It will also enhance your ability to provide meaningful one-another care in the local church.

Everyone has relationships and, in the course of those relationships, everyone experiences problems. Does Scripture have anything to say about how we approach one another in the mess of life? Of course it does! Scripture provides us with dozens and dozens of one-another commands, each with a unique directive for how we are called to love those around us. In *Loving Messy People*, the commands are summarized in these four categories: knowing, serving, speaking, and "gospeling." These are the biblical building blocks of all gospel care.

Each lesson in this *Intro to (Messy) Care and Discipleship* is designed to help you better understand how relationships work in the mess of life. You will discover and appreciate the beauty of God's design as he orchestrates relationships to transform his children into the image of his Son. You will consider some of the barriers that exist in one-another care as well as some of the opportunities. You will see the kindness of God as He approaches his people gently, and you will learn to desire what the Savior desires: that our relationships might reflect his perfect unity.

We recommend that you do this program in a group.[1] In his book *Compelling Community*, Jamie Dunlop describes the body of Christ working in tandem to evangelize an unbeliever. Dunlop calls this "mob evangelism"—every church member participating in the life of a person in need of hearing the good news. We believe the church would also benefit significantly from a practice of "mob discipleship." Paul tells us that each person has been given a gift for the building up of Christ's body (1 Cor. 12:4–6). God empowers every service and every activity. By studying how to love messy people in a group, you will begin to see how the Lord equips each of his children uniquely. You will then be able to put the things you're learning into practice immediately with the other members of your group.

## THE STRUCTURE OF THE STUDY GUIDE

During this course you will be asked to engage in loving messy people. This will involve observing both the positive and negative responses we all tend to exhibit in messy situations. By examining how you react to a mess, you will begin to identify the particular obstacles you are prone to encounter in gospel care. Together, we will discuss how to avoid these obstacles and respond to others in love, the way God has called us to.

Additionally, you will be encouraged to practice biblical gospel care with someone God has placed in your life. Please remember, however: the people to whom you purposefully minister are not projects! They are fellow image-bearers whom God has placed in your life for a purpose. They are the brothers and sisters that God is specifically calling you to love.

Between the sessions, you will be asked to read, reflect, and journal about the circumstances God has ordained in your life and how you have responded. While we can introduce you to the biblical principles of gospel care, the real work will occur in these times with the Lord. Take this opportunity to search God's Word, think, pray, and evaluate. It will be important to learn how to pay close attention to the guidance of the Holy Spirit as you love God's people.

It goes without saying that prayer is a huge factor in the journey ahead. Pray for yourself (for wisdom, discernment, compassion), but also pray for those you're called to love. You will want to spend much time before the Lord, allowing him to prepare your heart for the incredibly high calling of caring for one another. The people God has called us to help are both hurting and struggling. They may be suffering the worst kind of pain experienced in a fallen world; they may be struggling with the darkest depths of sin in their hearts. God is calling you to approach them with a genuine heart, softened by the Holy Spirit, prepared to mirror His love. Our prayer is that this course will help to provide that preparation.

Through this course our hope is that you will:

○ Discover the sweetness of gospel care.

○ Be empowered to embrace your call to minister to others in the mess life.

○ Learn how to lovingly minister to others in light of the gospel.

○ Gain confidence to minister to others when they are hurting, confused, or caught in sin.

○ Develop greater wisdom to address the multitude of different problems and situations that will arise in your own life and the lives of those around you.

○ Grow in love for those God has placed in your life.

## The Structure of the Course

*Intro to (Messy) Care and Discipleship* is designed to equip everyday Christians using four distinct tools:

○ Participants in small groups will be invited to view a teaching session in which Scott Mehl teaches an overview of the session's topic. Every member of the small group can follow along with an outline provided. There are eight teaching sessions in all.

○ After watching each teaching session, the small group will be invited to observe a roundtable discussion. These roundtable discussions are strategically comprised of pastors, elders, advocates, small group leaders, biblical counselors, and disciplers with years of experience in one-another care. The small group participants will "listen in" on these incredibly practical conversations, recognizing the common ground we all share as we succeed and fail to love fallen people in a fallen world. There is a total of eight roundtable discussions.

○ The small group will then initiate their own (guided) discussions about how they themselves approach knowing, serving, speaking, and gospeling as they strive to love messy people in their own lives. By working together through the **Group Discussion and Reflection** questions and **Digging into the Word** questions in this book, group members will gain practical and biblical guardrails for thinking about the dynamics of messy relationships.

○ Finally, in the **Putting It Into Practice** section, each participant will be given assignments designed to help them live out what they've learned in their various messy relationships.

This is a much-needed resource for the church that demystifies one-another care and equips every Christian to participate in the high calling of loving one another well.

# 1

## What is Gospel Care?

# The Calling of All Christians

○ *Gospel care is the God-exalting, grace-saturated art of loving another person, through patiently knowing, sacrificially serving, truthfully speaking, and consistently applying the gospel in order to help them become more like Jesus.*

## Story

### Christine Chappell

After the birth of our third child, depression hit me like a ton of bricks. While I was familiar with various highs and lows since I was a teenager, this season was particularly brutal because it was the most significant season of darkness I had walked through as a born-again believer in Christ. I was caught off guard by the severity of the sadness. My faith was still young and I had not experienced much in the way of personal suffering after I came to know the Lord. Those months wading through a deep sense of confusion taught me that I could not avoid suffering through an excess of faith—there was no single formula or Scripture verse or moral effort that could repair my crushed spirit.

During that time, my husband and I reached out to our pastor to help us navigate my fluctuating emotions and crippling disappointment. He had received some training in one-another care and agreed to walk alongside us. While our pastor didn't have answers to the precise reasons I seemed to be trapped in what John Bunyan would call "the Great Despond," he faithfully showed up at our doorstep week after week to encourage us with rich gospel consolations.

Our pastor acted as a mirror for us both, and through the work of the Holy Spirit's application of God's Word in our hearts, we began to recognize how we were responding in unhelpful ways. When there were sins to confess, he graciously showed us what true repentance looked like according to the instruction of the Word. When despair felt suffocating, he encouraged us to remember the humanity of Christ—the Man of Sorrows—who is well acquainted with grief and sympathetic toward our varied experiences of life lived in a fallen world.

When our weeks of meeting together found me unstuck from my sorrows, I found a friend who I could continue to pursue spiritual maturity with. The simplicity of our pastor's attention had a profound impact on the trajectory of my life. Never once did I believe he was showing up to "fix" my problem, but rather to point me to Christ, my Wonderful Counselor.

I can look back on this season of life and see how God's care was funneled through a man who committed to show up and help us look up to the ultimate Healer of our hearts for help.

The time I spent working through these issues with a friend watered the seeds our pastor had planted through his faithful one-another care. As we met weekly, we focused on what I *could do* in the midst of my depression, instead of the self-imposed belief that I had to "fix myself." I learned it was possible for me to *choose* to honor God with my life through humble service to my family; it was possible for me to *choose* to do the next right thing; it was possible for me to *choose* to hope in God for the present day, and to trust him for tomorrow.

These choices may not have immediately alleviated my experience of depression, but they did help me take courage and wait upon God for my joy to be restored. I began to view my chronic cycles of depression as a training ground for my faith instead of something strange or abnormal that was happening to me. Over time, by the gentle teaching of the Holy Spirit and the discipleship of faithful believers, I learned that my life did not have to be sorrow-free to be glorifying to God. In fact, God was revealing that I had made healing from depression an idol—something I required in order to experience joy, peace, and satisfaction in my life. Once I understood that my main motivation and purpose for living was to glorify God to the best of my ability—and rest in his grace when my abilities proved their eventual limitations—a load lifted off my shoulders. I wasn't called to fix myself. I was simply called to come to Christ, over and over again.

When I reflect on that season of life, I do not see the application of "solutions"—rather, I see the careful, compassionate application of the Scriptures in the life of a child of God. It was through this intentional discipleship period that I experienced what Romans 15:4 describes:

> *For everything that was written in the past*
> *was written to teach us, so that through the*
> *endurance taught in the Scriptures and the*
> *encouragement they provide we might have hope.*

The truth is, my pastor and my friend were instruments in the hands of God. They repeatedly heralded the gospel in the midst of my sorrows and taught me to make the Lord my one, true refuge. Through our fellowship time and prayer, I was shown how to view my challenges through a biblical lens. Their ministry to me in the midst of my pain was so meaningful, I became inspired to pursue training in biblical one-another care as well. Years after this experience, by God's grace, I'm leaning in to the divine design for Christian community by serving as a conduit of comfort to sufferers of depression. As 2 Corinthians 1:3–4 proclaims,

> *Praise be to the God and Father of our Lord Jesus*
> *Christ, the Father of compassion and the God of*
> *all comfort, who comforts us in all our troubles,*
> *so that we can comfort those in any trouble with*
> *the comfort we ourselves receive from God.*

## GROUP DISCUSSION AND REFLECTION

1.  As you read the story, does it remind you of a time when you were in a similar situation either as the giver of comfort or the recipient of care? Give a brief description here.

*Share your stories with the group.*

2.  What tends to hold you back from reaching out to others when your own life gets messy? Make a list.

3.  What tends to hold you back from stepping into the messy situations of others? Make a list.

*Share the top three things that tend to hold you back with the group.*

4. Write down some of the ways that other members in your group are held back.

   Chances are, we will all experience similar challenges when presented with an opportunity to give gospel care.

5. What are examples of the times you have responded positively to God's calling to provide gospel care to others? (List several examples.)

*Share one of these times with your group.*

## DIGGING INTO THE WORD

1.  Read Ephesians 4:7–16. Identify all of the gifts listed in these passages.

|  | For example: grace (according to Christ's gift) |
| --- | --- |
| 4:7 | |
| 4:8 | |
| 4:11 | |
| 4:11 | |
| 4:11 | |
| 4:11 | |
| 4:11 | |
| 4:13 | |
| 4:13 | |
| 4:13 | |
| 4:13 | |
| 4:14 | |
| 4:15 | |
| 4:16 | |

2. Why were the "office" gifts given to the church (4:12)?

2a. How do you view the responsibility of the "officers" of the church?

2b. Whom has God called to do the "work of ministry" in the church (pastors or all the "saints")?

2c. How should this shape our expectations for the church family?

2d. Did you know that God calls YOU to build his church?

2e. What do you think that looks like practically in your life?

3. What is the ultimate goal the ministry of the "saints" is working toward (see gifts above)?

4. What are some of the waves that toss people and carry them away from knowing and believing the truth?

5. What are the practical ways we (the "saints") can encourage our struggling brothers and sisters when they are tossed to and fro (4:14–15)?

6. What happens when the whole body works in unity, bonded together by the gracious gifts of God?

## For Additional Study

Identify the spiritual blessings in Ephesians 1–3 that equip the saints for the work of ministry.

*See Appendix 1*

Identify the blessings God gives his people listed in Psalm 68. Paul references these gifts when he encourages the church in Ephesus.

*See Appendix 2*

## Putting It Into Practice—Homework

God loves when we love his children. He asks us to step into the "messy" lives of others both actively and practically. He even tells us that it is through our love for one another that we come to know him better (1 John 4:7). It is a gift, in and of itself, that he has invited us to take part in the care of his people—just as it is a gift that he's provided others to take part in caring for us.

Time and again, we neglect this gift because it feels "too hard" or we don't "know enough" to help. But the truth is, God has graciously given us all the tools we need to care for one another. He simply asks us to obey his commands to love others for the sake of his glory, our sanctification, and the benefit of his children. As with any seemingly daunting task, it's helpful to outline several achievable steps.

First, begin by identifying whom God has put in your life that he is calling you to care for and minister to.

Most of us have several people in our lives who could use gospel care. If you are having a hard time thinking of someone in need of care, it's possible you are keeping your relationships at a surface level. If that's the case, pray that the Lord would help spark increasingly genuine conversations between you and others in your life. And pray that he would give you eyes to see and ears to hear the needs of others.

If a person's name comes to mind, write their name in the blank space below.

_____ *is in need of gospel-care.*

I will commit to caring for this person in any way that I am able.

Contact this person to tell them you're praying for them. Ask how you can care for them. Take the time to fill out the following questions after your conversation.

APPLICATION

1. What are some of the hurts, struggles, or areas of confusion this person has communicated to you?

2. What are some of the ways you could care for them that they have communicated to you?

3. What are some of the ways you could care for them that you can anticipate, even if they haven't explicitly communicated about them?

4. Do they need a listening ear?

## Acts of Love

1. Could they use some financial help? Would they benefit from help with a résumé or a budget?

2. Could they use some practical help with cleaning their home, household repairs, or childcare?

3. What gifts has the Lord given to you that might help you meet the needs of this person?

4. Even if you aren't adept at cooking, you may have a ministry at your church that can provide meals. Do you have the financial flexibility to order a meal delivered? If their issue is the struggle to make ends meet, do you know how to help them organize their finances or create a budget? Do you have a connection that could open the door for them to find a more suitable job? Brainstorm some ideas below:

| Need | Gift |
|------|------|
|      |      |
|      |      |
|      |      |
|      |      |
|      |      |

5. If there are needs that you are unable to meet, whom could you contact to help? As an example, maybe you are not able to help your friend with home repairs, but you know a person at your church who is. Maybe you can't offer childcare, but your college-aged daughter would be willing to help. Brainstorm some ideas below:

| Need | Contact | Contact Information |
|---|---|---|
| | | |
| | | |
| | | |
| | | |

## WORDS OF LOVE

1. Does their heart need some encouragement and affirmation for how they are striving to follow Christ?

2. Is there a particular or glaring sin issue that needs to be confronted or addressed?

3. Is there a truth about God that they need to be reminded of, even if they know it already?

4. What biblical truths do you know that might help point this person back to Christ?

5. In addition to practical needs, how can you minister to your friend spiritually? What kind of passages might encourage them? What characteristics of the Lord would bring them comfort? List at least two passages of Scripture and two characteristics of the Lord to share with your friend below.

| Scripture Passage | Characteristics of the Lord |
| --- | --- |
| | |
| | |
| | |
| | |
| | |
| | |

6.  What do you know about these passages and character traits? Consider how these truths have ministered to you in times of difficulty. Write some of your ideas below and make it a point to share these truths.

---

Schedule a time to meet face-to-face with the friend with whom you've committed to give care. It can be as simple as a get-together at a coffee shop or hanging out after the kids are in bed. Maybe it would work better to meet at one of your homes. It may even be more effective to talk as you participate in an activity, such as walking or doing yard work. However you choose to meet, make sure to get a time on your calendar.

Next time you meet together with your study group, plan on discussing some of the results of your assignment. Please, always be cautious to share only what information is appropriate without revealing anything that should remain confidential. This is a great opportunity to learn from others in your study group about the unique and creative ways God is using them in the lives of those around them. We've all been called to the same kind of care, but no two relationships will ever be exactly the same.

## Prayer Prompts

○   Pray that God would help you as you seek to obey his call to love those he's placed in your life.

○   Pray that God would bring to mind those around you that would benefit from gospel care.

○   Pray that, through this process, you would grow in love for God and love for others.

○   Pray that the Lord would sanctify you through this process and make you become more like Christ.

# THE ART OF GOSPEL CARE

- *Gospel care is more of an art than a science. There's no script.*
- *Gospel care isn't like playing a fully orchestrated piece of music with every note in its proper place and every twist and turn predetermined.*
- *Gospel care is like jazz. It's fluid, unpredictable, surprising, and unique every time.*
- *Learning to minister to others is like learning any other improvisational art. You need to know the basics well, but you need to maintain the flexibility to adjust and respond lovingly in each different situation, because they will all be unique.*

## STORY

### ANN MAREE GOUDZWAARD, CINDY STASHENKO

I met her in a small, loud coffee shop near the neighborhood where I lived. The tables were jam packed together and the air smelled like burnt coffee. I wondered if we would be able to have a private conversation.

Cindy was twenty-seven years old and single. She had just recently started attending my church. Cindy said she was happy to find a church where she could hide and just listen. She said she would have been content to stay anonymous had it not been for her recent struggle with anxiety.

Her difficulty started several months back, she said. It was so severe that it got to the point of panic attacks. Cindy told me she feared for her safety (as well as the safety of others) because she was a nurse.

She looked at me with eyes worn and tired from countless sleepless nights and said she felt like she had hit rock bottom.

Since Cindy was new to our church, I knew nothing of her past or present situation. So, I listened as she shared her background and story. As she spoke, however, I tried to formulate an approach that would minister to her difficulties. I pondered what Scripture passages about anxiety I might share.

She said she came from a broken home. Cindy's mom left her dad when she was just three years old, and the man her mother remarried became her legal father. She told me her biological dad died in a car accident when she was eight.

Cindy said she remembered asking the Lord into her heart numerous times as a young child; her desire was to follow God. But no significant transformation ever happened, so she wondered what it was about her that seemed to prevent Christ from *sticking*. She was constantly obsessed with the thought that God would not accept her. Eventually someone told her, "You just needed to believe." So, Cindy believed the Lord for her salvation, quit asking him to save her, and was baptized at age twelve.

"High school and college were turbulent years," Cindy said. Her mind seemed farther away as she described a long-lost relationship with a young man in high school. Cindy was convinced at the time that he was "the one." Over their years together they became more intimate than they should have, and Cindy started drifting from the Lord.

*Ding, ding, ding!* There you have it. My ears perked up and I paid closer attention. "Peel that onion!" I could hear my mentor say. "There's always something behind the sinful behavior." Of course Cindy is anxious, I thought to myself. It is a fearful thing to fall into the hands of the living God. No wonder this woman is scared.

"Go on," I heard myself say. But in my head, I started adapting my previously planned agenda. I knew I would need to ask Cindy additional questions like, "Who moved, you or God?" And, "What does it look like to love God?" And, "Who does God make friends with?"

Cindy continued her story.

She said she attended church less and less during her college years and then moved far from her church home and family shortly after graduation. Since she also parted ways with her first boyfriend, she entered into another relationship. This new boyfriend added to the decline of her relationship with the Lord. She (by her own admission) walked further and further away from God.

Initially, Cindy said it was easy to blame her distance from God on her need to sort out her beliefs. In reality, the truth was that conviction was inconvenient. She no longer wanted to manage the guilt associated with her life choices. Cindy said she eventually turned her back on religion altogether and pursued a secular worldview that worshipped freedom, independence, and worldly enlightenment.

"Well," I thought to myself. "This is a no-brainer. Cindy just needs to get back into a right relationship with the Father." But right before I was about to "minister the word" to Cindy and show her from Scripture what might be creating her anxiety, a question I hadn't thought of yet crossed my mind.

"Cindy," I asked, "are you living with your boyfriend?"

Tears started to flow and Cindy slowly nodded her head. She then began crying uncontrollably. I handed her some tissues, but I was taken aback by such an intense response. I didn't even need to ask anything, though. Through her sobs, the next words out of her mouth were, "I had an abortion."

Silence. That was probably what the Lord wanted from me in the first place, but silence was the only response I could think of at that moment. I'd actually never spoken with someone who had an abortion, at least not to my knowledge. I couldn't imagine what goes through the mind of someone who feels so desperate and hopeless they would choose something so difficult.

I let Cindy continue.

Through gasps for air between her sobs, Cindy told me she felt she had no choice. She was stuck in a tiny house in an impoverished neighborhood with nowhere to go. The pregnancy was an unthinkable bombshell. Cindy had been on birth control for seven years but she had recently taken an antibiotic (treatment for a questionable STD), not realizing it might decrease the effectiveness of birth control. The first thought she had when she realized the possibility was, "I can't be pregnant." She even prayed for the first time in a long time; "Please, Lord . . . do not let me be pregnant." But when she went to Planned Parenthood, she found out it was true; Cindy was expecting a baby.

The air between us felt solemn. The anguish Cindy carried on her entire body was tangible. She was slumped over and she could barely look up. Shame seemed to envelop her. What do you say to someone who has experienced such pain? I surely didn't know.

I looked at the door. I looked at the clock. I looked at anything and everything except into Cindy's eyes. To say I could think of nothing to tell her is an understatement.

I silently prayed.

It took a few moments, but the Lord graciously reminded me of his words in Psalm 32. I asked Cindy if she wouldn't mind if I read it. She nodded, so I pulled it up on my phone and began to read.

Suddenly, I was the one choking back tears. . .

> *Blessed is the one whose transgression is forgiven, whose sin is covered. Blessed is the man against whom the LORD counts no iniquity, and in whose spirit there is no deceit.*
>
> *For when I kept silent, my bones wasted away through my groaning all day long. For day and night your hand was heavy upon me; my strength was dried up as by the heat of summer.*
>
> *I acknowledged my sin to you, and I did not cover my iniquity; I said, "I will confess my transgressions to the LORD," and you forgave the iniquity of my sin. Therefore, let everyone who is godly offer prayer to you at a time when you may be found; surely in the rush of great waters, they shall not reach him.*
>
> *You are a hiding place for me; you preserve me from trouble; you surround me with shouts of deliverance.*
>
> *Selah*
>
> *(Psalm 32:1–7)*

## GROUP DISCUSSION AND REFLECTION

1. What happens when you treat gospel care like a formulaic science?

*Share with your group a time when you fell into that trap.*

2. How do you deal with the fear that comes when you realize that there's no script, and yet God still wants you to care for and minister to others?

3. Can you think of a time the Spirit of God gave you wisdom, insight, or brought a truth to mind as you stepped into someone else's messy life? Describe the situation.

4. When you trust in your own wisdom and strength (instead of God's), how does it impact your relationships with others?

5. When you trust in the Lord for wisdom and strength, how does it shape your relationships with others?

*Share with the group a time you found yourself trusting the Lord or yourself when you were trying to care for someone.*

6. Write down some of the things that other members in your group share. Chances are, we will all experience similar challenges and victories.

## Digging into the Word

1. Read Philippians 1:1–17.
2. How did Paul feel about the church in Philippi?

*Paul thinks of them often with Joy and thankfulness to God*

---

2a. When you think about your immediate family, church family, and friends, what are some thoughts and feelings that come to mind? *That I love them and would do what I could to help them.*

---

2b. What did Paul hope for this church?

---

2c. What did Paul say advanced the gospel?

---

2d. We often make plans when we think about caring for a friend in a messy situation—for example, what we might say or how we need to approach them. What character trait does God tend to use in these relationships, rather than a simple "script"?

3. How did the gospel inform Paul's words?

4. What is the right way to "preach the gospel" (according to this passage)?

5. What is the wrong way (according to this passage)?

## For Additional Study

1.  Read Philippians 2:1–8, 12.
2.  Make a list of all the instructions Paul lists for how to approach one another in care.

| Verse | Action |
|---|---|
| 1 | |
| 1 | |
| 1 | |
| 1 | |
| 2 | |
| 2 | |
| 2 | |
| 3 | |
| 3 | |
| 3 | |
| 3 | |
| 4 | |
| 4 | |
| 5 | |
| 6 | |
| 7, 8 | |
| 12 | |

## Putting It Into Practice—Homework

As a child, you think mom or dad have all the answers, so you continually run to them for guidance. Mothers often joke about getting tired of hearing "Mom!" shouted over and over again, because their child continually needs them. As you get older and a bit more self-reliant, you're less likely to run to mom and dad for help. Teenagers might turn to their friends or the Internet. Adults might turn to their spouses or rely on their own experiences for understanding. Of course, relying completely on any of these sources for knowledge can be faulty. But the instinct to run to a higher authority is common to each of us. We all realize that we are not equipped to deal with all the issues that come with life.

When we stand face-to-face with a hurting friend who is sharing their pain, regret, or shame, it seems that it would be nice to have a script. Instead of a script, the Lord offers us a number of things to minister to his people—two of which are his sufficient Word, the Bible, and his Spirit who dwells in us. These gifts he gives us are better than a script.

Use the following homework assignment to assess the care you've been offering to the person you committed to in Chapter 1.

### Application

How did your initial meeting with your friend go? Were you able to meet any of their initial needs or create a plan to meet those needs? Did you learn of any additional cares this person might be burdened by? Do you have any thoughts about how you might be able to minister to this person with your specific giftings? Jot down your thoughts below.

1.   Needs met:

2. Plans created:

3. Burdens faced:

4. Helpful gifts:

5. What truth have you shared with your friend? Write the truths you shared below. If possible, write a Scripture reference that supports the truth you shared. A truth can be as simple as "I care for you and want to help you through this" (Phil. 1:3–11). Or, "even though I don't know what to say right now, I know that the Lord offers wisdom in this situation" (Phil. 1:6).

   5a. Truth shared:

5b. Scripture references:

6. Many times, the Lord uses things we've learned recently
to help us to minister to others. In his second letter to the
Corinthians, Paul notes that the comfort God offers us is
not meant simply for our own comfort. It's given to us so
that we may offer others comfort as well. He writes, "Blessed
be . . . the God of all comfort, who comforts us in all our
affliction, so that we may be able to comfort those who
are in any affliction" (2 Cor. 1:3–5). We are meant to "share
abundantly in comfort" with those around us. Consider the
ways you have been comforted by God recently in your own
life. It could be from learning about God through a sermon,
a book, or your own time in the Bible. How might you use
that comfort to minister to your friend?

6a. Truths learned:

6b. Scripture references:

7. Schedule a time to meet personally with your friend again. Write down the date and time on your calendar, as well as in the space below.

## Prayer Prompts

- Pray that your recent comfort from God might be used to comfort your friend.
- Pray that you will be able to help meet your friend's needs.
- Pray that the Lord will teach you about his character and that it might be useful to your friend.
- Pray that your friend would find comfort in the burdens of this life, both through your loving ministry and God's presence.
- Pray that you would be open to Spirit-empowered improvisation, rather than being tied to a script for caring for your friend.

# The Centrality of Love

○ *Every aspect of gospel care is an application of the second greatest commandment:*

○ *"You shall love your neighbor as yourself" (Matt. 22:39).*

○ *The centrality of love in personal ministry can go without saying but, too often, that is exactly the problem.*

○ *Love is not simply a prerequisite to good ministry; love is good ministry.*

○ *Without love all of our best efforts to minister to one another are worthless (1 Cor. 13).*

○ *But with love, gospel care produces a beautiful, powerful, dynamic relationship that blesses the recipient and glorifies the Creator.*

## Story

### Anna Mondal

*I can't keep living like this.* I was sprawled out on my living room floor (again) after another overwhelming day of meetings with people. I know ministry is tough, but are you supposed to feel like you've been run over by a truck at the end of every single day? My days were a whirlwind of sessions, follow-ups, phone calls, notes, extra meetings, emails, texts, and lots of Kleenex boxes. After the third person told me something to the effect of, "Wow, you put your whole heart into it," I started to wonder if ministry was meant to have my whole heart. If ministry has my heart—my best attention, time, energy, resources, and focus—

maybe it's turning into something godlike, something that would eat me alive if I worshipped it.

If you asked me what my motivation was, I would say, "Love for people!" And that was partly true. But my day was actually shaped more by fear than love. My schedule was driven by the needs of other people: I began my day by checking email, making to-do lists, reassuring and responding to people who "needed" me, fitting in new appointments even if I had no comfortable space left in my day, sacrificing my time in personal study and reflection to make time for other people. I was motivated by a desire to feel important, successful, and helpful. It felt like love ("I'm available! I'm helpful! I say yes when you need me!"), but it wasn't. It left me self-reliant, fatigued, and uncompassionate toward others (who invariably didn't praise me for twisting into a pretzel to accommodate their needs). It left me wanting to quit ministry forever and take up FedEx driving (which for me, as a former classical ballerina, wouldn't have been a great fit).

So, naturally, I decided that I wasn't cut out for this; I couldn't love people. It was too hard.

From my literal and metaphorical face-plant, I asked for help. I cried to God, cried to my husband, and talked to a small cadre of wise friends. It slowly dawned on me that this wasn't "ministry burnout" or compassion fatigue. Not exactly. I was exhausted because I was attempting the impossible—I was trying to be the source of love. I was spending from an empty account.

Through exhaustion, humiliation, and a lot of time alone with the Lord, I remembered (and experienced) real love all over again. God showed me what love looked like—because he is love itself. God is love itself. And he says that I can only love because he loved me first. I knew that, I taught that, I loved that truth. But I functionally forgot it. I lived as a person unloved—a person wholly responsible to love others from my own capabilities and energy. But God's words brought me freedom, and beckoned me beautifully—*you love because I first loved you . . . when you love me and remain in my love, you love my children* (John 15:4; 1 John 4:19; 5:2).

I still spend time with people dizzied by fear of failing. I still fight sinful tendencies to overexert, overcommit, and be overly responsible. But I'm fighting differently now. One of the most important changes I've made to my schedule is establishing a new morning ritual. I don't take appointments before 9 A.M. I don't start by checking email, making to-do lists, running through my schedule, and tapping out text replies. I don't let my mind go wild with my responsibilities and tasks and hopes and fears for the day. Unless I have an urgent message from someone who is suicidal, I ignore everything until I soak in God's presence. I sit in my chair, all alone, and spend time praying, meditating, and reading Scripture—for *myself*. I receive before I give. I abide in love before I try to show love.

I've noticed that when I spend more time contemplating God's love rather than hammering out a plan, I'm far more prepared to enter caregiving in a spirit of genuine love. I'm learning to acknowledge my limits, and say no to people. I'm learning to mess up without being totally crushed. I'm learning to be genuinely myself, because I remember who I am (a conduit, not source, of love) and I remember who God is (love itself). I'm more excited about the real Messiah, and less inclined to play the role of mini-messiah. My anchor isn't my own energy, love, or likeability, but rather God's love: "Abide in my love . . . without me you can do nothing" (John 15:5, 9).

## GROUP DISCUSSION AND REFLECTION

1.  What, other than love, might motivate you to step into someone else's mess?

*Share with your group a time when that motivation propelled you into someone else's life.*

2.  How did that other motivation negatively impact the way you ministered to or cared for them?

3.  What, practically, can you do in order to keep genuine love as the motivation of your ministry to others?

4. What are some of the manifestations of genuine love we should expect to see in our ministry to others?

5. Write down some of the things that other members in your group share.

## DIGGING INTO THE WORD

1. Read 1 John 4:7–5:2.
2. Why does John say we should love one another?

---

3. What are the implications if someone does not exhibit love toward their neighbor?

---

4. What is love?

---

5. What sustains your love for others?

---

6.  How does genuine love manifest in our emotions? In our thoughts? In our actions?

7.  How does John tell us that people will see the evidence of the Holy Spirit in our lives?

8.  Anyone can love. What makes the Christian's love different?

9.  What is the significance of the word "abiding" in verses 15 and 16?

10. Look up John 15:4–15. In that passage, what are the positive and negative consequences of either abiding or not abiding?

| Positive consequences | Negative consequences |
| --- | --- |
|  |  |
|  |  |
|  |  |
|  |  |
|  |  |

## FOR ADDITIONAL STUDY

We rightly feel the burden of our loved ones' problems and are eager to help. However, often our desires turn in on themselves. We feel as though *we* are the ones responsible for fixing their problems and saving them from suffering or rescuing them from sin. This kind of "Savior complex" is a trap; it's the opposite of Christ's calling.

List what Christ has done for us from Isaiah 53:2–12. Make note of the ways in which this demonstrates how impossible it is for you to try to do the work of the Savior.

| Verse | Christ's calling | Struggle |
|-------|------------------|----------|
| 2 | | |
| 3 | | |
| 3 | | |
| 3 | | |
| 3 | | |
| 3 | | |
| 4 | | |
| 4 | | |
| 4 | | |
| 5 | | |
| 5 | | |
| 5 | | |
| 5 | | |
| 6 | | |
| 7 | | |
| 7 | | |
| 7 | | |
| 8 | | |
| 8 | | |
| 8 | | |
| 9 | | |
| 9 | | |
| 10 | | |
| 10 | | |
| 10 | | |
| 11 | | |
| 12 | | |

## Putting It Into Practice—Homework

Love is central to one-another ministry. Without true, biblical love, we easily come up short and get burnt out as we minister to others. We begin to feel frustrated by the mess of others' lives. And we ultimately become overwhelmed and hopeless. Thankfully, in Christ, God has given us all that we need to truly and genuinely love others. He outlines the "why," the "how," and the "what" of love clearly in his Word—"We love because he first loved us" (1 John 4:19).

Consider the depth of the love of God. Read Romans 11:33 to 11:36. What does this tell you about the love of God? List your thoughts below.

...................................................................................................................

...................................................................................................................

...................................................................................................................

...................................................................................................................

...................................................................................................................

As you love and minister to the person you identified in chapter 1 (or to others), it's imperative that you do so out of an overflow of God's love for you. He has offered us his Spirit, his Word, and his people to teach us more about his character and love. This week, read, study, and pray using the following passages. Write out some of the descriptions of God's love from each passage. Take some time to consider how each description can motivate you to love the person (or people) you are striving to minister to. Seek to call these truths to mind as you minister to your friend.

- ○ Psalm 34
- ○ Psalm 86
- ○ Romans 5:1–11
- ○ 1 John 3:1–3
- ○ 1 John 4:7–21

| What does this passage say about God's love? | How can this motivate me to love others? |
|---|---|
| Example: The Lord hears his people. | *I can turn to the Lord with my burdens and he will care for me. He is with me, even if I feel overwhelmed. If my friend shares her burdens with me, I can help her turn to the Lord as well.* |
| | |
| | |
| | |
| | |

## Prayer Prompts

As you minister to your friend this week, consider praying through the following prompts:

- Pray that you would grow in love for God by learning more about his loving character.
- Pray that God's love for you would motivate you to love others.
- Pray that you'd find willingness to sacrifice for your friends in the sacrificial love of Christ.
- Pray that you would rely on God for help, rather than being self-reliant as you minister to others.
- Pray that your friend would ultimately find help and hope in God and not in you.

# 2

How Do We Patiently Know?

# KNOWING ONE ANOTHER

○ *Even when we love someone, we can't minister to them effectively if we haven't taken the time to truly know them. The first step in knowing another person is to consistently, patiently, and sincerely listen to them. We live in a time and place where everyone is talking, but few people are truly listening. To minister in the midst of the mess, we must first learn to listen, ask good questions, and then listen some more.*

## STORY

### NATE BROOKS

I had seen the Holy Spirit convict, transform, and heal situations far worse than the one sitting in front facing me, so there didn't appear to be anything insurmountable. Sean and Hayden were very involved in our church; they regularly sat under good, biblical preaching. By all accounts, the deck was stacked in their favor. When we started talking about the difficulties in their marriage, I had high hopes. Yes, there was a variety of problems produced by years of sin on top of sin. But that was always the case with long-standing conflict.

Our times together started out well; it only took a couple meetings before everyone agreed on the primary problems in the marriage. Both Sean and Hayden were willing to own their own contribution to the strife that consumed their household. Both were committed to de-escalating the conflict. Most importantly, both agreed on the solution.

As we continued meeting over the weeks, Sean and Hayden recognized the gospel implications for their marriage and knew the Spirit would help them. Yet neither of them changed. Hayden waited for Sean to make the first move; Sean held his posture of, "I'll change when she does." They were at an impasse.

My optimism quickly faded and, instead of patiently understanding this struggling couple, I grew angry.

Our get-togethers became an iceberg on my calendar, an object of dread. I found it more and more difficult to concentrate when we met. My own internal monologue of "Don't yell at them" rose in volume. I'm not always the brightest bulb in the pack, but I concluded that yelling things like, "Why can't you just be more like Jesus!" didn't seem like it would be particularly helpful.

So, I prayed for God's grace to get my own heart where it ought to be. How did I get to a place where all I wanted to do was yell at this dear couple sitting in front of me?

Our hearts are always a mix of impulses. There was some good in my heart when I grew angry. Sean and Hayden were dishonoring God. But if I'm honest, a concern for their holiness was not what pushed me over the edge. God showed me that I was mainly angry at this couple because their refusal to change messed up my day and often even messed up my week.

I became impatient and frustrated with the inconvenience of loving messy people.

Some messy people will change; others won't. It's impossible to tell who will and who won't, because it's impossible to truly know a person's heart ahead of time. Regardless, I am called to exhibit the fruit of the Spirit in love. Love is patient, love is kind, and I was neither of those things. In hindsight, I realized I need the Holy Spirit actively working in my own heart as much as the people I'm seeking to help. Loving messy people is always hard. It requires God's grace to develop the discipline of listening, genuine care and concern, and gospel-shaped patience with the process. Just as those we're called to minister to need to change, God is in the process of changing us, too.

## GROUP DISCUSSION AND REFLECTION

1. What makes a good listener?

*Share with your group how you have succeeded or failed at this in the past.*

2. How do you know what questions to ask?

3. What happens in our relationships when we don't interpret what others are telling us from a biblical worldview?

4. Why is taking time to "consider what's most needed" so incredibly important?

*Share with your group personal stories that demonstrate why it's so important.*

5. What precedes loving someone well?

6. Write down some of the things that other members in your group share. Chances are, we will all experience similar challenges and victories.

## Digging into the Word

1. Proverbs is full of passages that teach us about the importance of listening well. Summarize the main point of each of the following proverbs, and then make a list of what you learn about patient listening from them.

   1a. Proverbs 10:19

   1b. Proverbs 12:18

   1c. Proverbs 15:28

   1d. Proverbs 17:27

1e.  Proverbs 18:13

1f.  Proverbs 18:17

1g.  Proverbs 20:5

2.  How would applying the truth of this proverb help you to listen, ask questions, or know others better?

   *If one gives an answer before he hears, it is his folly and shame (Proverbs 18:13).*

3. Which of these proverbs do you need to remember the most? Memorize it!

4. Where else in Scripture might expand on the truth mentioned in this proverb?

   *The heart of the righteous ponders how to answer but the mouth of the wicked pours out evil things Proverbs 15:28).*

5. How might the relationships you're in now be impacted if you applied the truth of this proverb?

   *The purpose in a man's heart is like deep water, but a man of understanding will draw it out (Proverbs 20:5).*

## Putting It Into Practice—Homework

In his letters, Paul repeatedly called his recipients "beloved." He deeply loved those he ministered to. We can see the depth of his love not only from his continual declarations of love, but also by the ways in which he understood those he ministered to. He was able to both encourage and admonish them insightfully. He knew their tendencies, their strengths, and their worries.

Even more so, Christ showed love to his disciples by knowing them deeply. Christ was able to discern the thoughts of his disciples and comfort them according to their specific worries (John 16:19). He knew them well enough to know the information they would be able to handle (John 16:13). He was skilled at speaking the right truth at the right time.

So often, this is not the case with us. We're quick to offer opinions or platitudes that give little comfort. We'd rather take the shortcut to fixing people's problems than dwell in the mess and sort through it with them. But, to actively love someone, it's important to spend time getting to truly know them.

## Application

1.  Take some time to briefly summarize the situation of the friend you have committed to minister to. What are some victories they've had? What about setbacks? How have you sought to serve them? What truth have you shared with them?

2.  Now, take some time to evaluate. Have the actions you've taken or the truth you've shared been "what's most needed"? Before you acted or spoke, did you take time to ask them questions and truly listen to them?

3. Consider the following areas people commonly make assumptions about as they minister to others. Circle areas in which you may be assuming you know about your friend, but you've never actually asked:

- ○ Understanding of the gospel
- ○ Testimony of salvation
- ○ Experience of hardship
- ○ Lack or existence of trauma in life
- ○ Beliefs about God's character
- ○ Difficult relationships
- ○ Desire for repentance
- ○ Intention behind words and actions
- ○ Other: _____

4. For any categories that you've circled, seek to understand this person rather than just making assumptions. Use the list of questions below as inspiration for general guidance on what might be helpful to ask when you meet next.

4a. How does the gospel affect your day-to-day life?

4b. What experience has shaped you the most in life?

4c. Do you feel that you're tempted to behave in a certain way due to past experiences?

4d. What three words would you use to describe God?

4e. What do you believe is most important about relationships?

5. Have you committed the "God-ignoring error?" In other words, have you offered abundant pragmatic advice without consulting the Word of God for answers? Take some time to reflect on ways you may or may not have used God-centered, biblical wisdom as an answer for your friend's problems. In ways you've neglected God's wisdom, commit to offering it to your friend the next time you meet. What biblical wisdom could you offer in place of the advice you've given?

| Pragmatic Advice | Biblical Wisdom |
| --- | --- |
| | |
| | |
| | |
| | |
| | |
| | |
| | |
| | |

## PRAYER PROMPTS

This week, consider the following as you pray for your friend:

- Pray that you will love your friend by seeking to know them.
- Pray that your friend would be willing to share with you openly.
- Pray and thank God for his deep understanding of you. Ask God to let that motivate you to learn more about the people you minister to.
- Pray that you'd avoid the temptation to "fix" problems with pragmatic advice rather than biblical wisdom.
- Pray that you'd be quick to rely on God for wisdom, rather than your own ideas.
- Thank God for his work in both you and your friend through this process.

# 3

## What Is Sacrificial Serving?

# Serving One Another

- *Somehow, somewhere along the way, personal ministry (discipling, mentoring, counseling, etc.) became primarily about talking to one another.*

- *When we think about ministering to others, we usually picture two people sitting in an office or at a coffee shop talking about life, issues, Scripture, God, and the gospel.*

- *But while gospel care must at least involve speaking the truth, it must involve more.*

- *We are also called to serve those we minister to practically and sacrificially.*

## Story

### Scott Mehl

Things had spiraled out of control for Lorenzo. He had always struggled with depression, differing forms of anxiety, and lack of motivation at work. But this was different. Lately he had been having trouble even getting out of bed in the morning. He would sit at his desk for hours and hours, just staring at the screen, refreshing his favorite news sites over and over again. Nothing seemed to matter. He didn't really seem to care. Everything was just gray and dark. Lorenzo was numb. And the people around him had begun to notice.

His wife noticed, and tried in multiple ways to get him to talk about how he was feeling. His small group noticed, and once spent an entire meeting letting him share and praying for him. His friends noticed and began pursuing him more regularly. His pastors noticed and reached out to offer comfort, counsel, and help.

But the spiral just continued and continued. Multiple times I got a call or text from Lorenzo's wife saying that she didn't know where he was or that he hadn't come home until late into the night. His drinking ramped up as his heart spiraled down, which only complicated the situation. And Lorenzo began to confess to those closest to him that he was struggling to find a reason to live and that things would probably just be easier if he were to take his own life.

It was at this point that I knew it was "all hands on deck." I didn't know exactly what Lorenzo needed, or how I could help, but I joined the chorus of people reaching out to him, and the two of us began meeting together weekly to talk about life, God, and the hopelessness that seemed to have consumed him.

On the face of it, Lorenzo really struggled to identify where the hopelessness was coming from. He had four beautiful children who all loved him. He and his wife had their struggles, like all couples, but overall they had a strong marriage. Lorenzo was employed. He had friends. He was well liked, respected, and loved. The hopelessness didn't seem to make any sense.

But the more we talked, the more the subtle contributors to Lorenzo's hopelessness rose to the surface. It wasn't just one thing (because it's never just one thing), but there was a litany of forces contributing to Lorenzo's downward spiral. There was his unhealthy eating and exercise habits. There was a difficult and complicated relationship with his parents. There was the mid-life realization that certain dreams and expectations were most likely not going to be fulfilled. There was a subtle, self-pitying heart response. And, much, much more.

But there was one theme in particular that seemed to come up again and again—one theme that tracked between his relationship with his parents and his attitude toward work and his disappointments with his living situation: money. Money was one of the subtle loves that deeply shaped Lorenzo's worldview, and that was a consistent determiner, in the depth of his heart, of what was really real.

One day I got a panicked call from Lorenzo's wife who knew he was in a particularly dark place, and couldn't get ahold of him. I tried texting Lorenzo and I tried calling him, but he wouldn't respond to me either. So, I got in my car and headed over to Lorenzo's office. I knew that Lorenzo worked in an office alone (being self-employed), and I was worried about him. When I got there, to my relief, Lorenzo answered the intercom and let me in.

We talked for a while about how he was doing, and our conversation meandered all over the place. But finally Lorenzo broke down and confessed to me the thing that had triggered this dive into darkness. His wife had asked for clarity about their financial situation, needing to make a couple of purchases, and Lorenzo froze. He responded in anger, and he stormed out of the house. His head had been spinning ever since. He was panicked and confused, and he didn't know what to do. You see, unknown to anyone, Lorenzo hadn't looked at his bank account in over three months. He had no idea what kind of financial situation he was actually in.

As Lorenzo talked, I simply listened. Lorenzo works on commission and the invoices he sends out get paid at all different frequencies. But he had been so paralyzed by the fear of not having enough money that he had simply stopped looking at his bank account altogether. At this point, months had gone by and he truly had no idea what kind of financial situation his family was in.

After listening for a long time, instead of telling Lorenzo what he should do, or how he should think, I simply offered to look at the account online together with him. I told him that whatever the number was, we would work through it together. And, even more importantly, whatever the number was, God was going to take care of his family and was going to answer his prayer for daily bread.

After about ten minutes of considering my offer, Lorenzo and I bowed our heads, prayed (thanking God for his faithfulness and asking for Lorenzo and his family's daily bread), and then Lorenzo logged on and, together, we looked at the status of his account.

To Lorenzo's surprise the account wasn't overdrawn. In fact, it had a decent amount of money in it. So we immediately went back to prayer, thanking God for his goodness and his provision. We prayed for God's help for courage and strength as well.

In the months following that moment, Lorenzo (slowly but surely) continued to grow and be strengthened by the love of God. His finances took some pretty bad hits after that, but his response was subtly different every time. God was growing a deepening trust in Lorenzo's heart that could only come from the work of the Spirit.

But when Lorenzo looks back at the catalyst of that moment in his office, the thing that sticks with him, and that was shocking to his soul, wasn't actually the fact that there was money in his bank account. The thing that shocked him that day was the fact that I didn't judge him and criticize him for having not looked at his bank account for months at a time. He knew it was irresponsible, but he couldn't understand why I didn't lay into him for his irresponsibility.

It was that grace-filled, gentle response that opened his eyes to see, in a new way, the grace-filled gentle responses he had been receiving from so many different people in his life. His wife, his friends, his fellow small-group members. All of them had been showing him this same kind of grace, and with new eyes he was coming to understand the beauty and the power of the grace of God in the gospel.

Lorenzo knew the truth of the gospel; he had been taught it regularly since he was little. He could recite the gospel message perfectly to anyone who asked him, but there were ways that it hadn't quite sunk down into his heart yet. And the thing Lorenzo needed more than anything that day, in that moment of panic and fear, wasn't for the gospel message to be told to him again, but for it to be shown to him in tangible living color. It was an act of service, not a spoken word, that God used to break through into Lorenzo's heart that day. Because sometimes, like Jesus, the most powerful communicator of love is what we *do*.

## GROUP DISCUSSION AND REFLECTION

1.  Is there a time in your life when another Christian did something for you (an act of service) in a way that brought the truth of the gospel to life?

*Share that circumstance with your group.*

2. We tend to think of gospel care as primarily a "talking" ministry. How have you seen loving relationships in the local church involve action, not just words?

   2a. Compare some of those actions with other members in your group.

3. How regularly do you pray for those you're ministering to?

   3a. What happens when we fail to pray?

4. In *Loving Messy People,* Scott describes what people often call "church discipline" as ultimately "church pursuit." But God has called his church to be pursuing one another even before life gets particularly messy. Explain to your group some of the ways in which you can pursue others when . . .

   4a. . . . their life is going well

   4b. . . . their life is not going well

   4c. . . . they "go quiet"

   4d. . . . they're caught in sin

5. Write down some of the things that other members in your group share. Chances are, we will all experience similar situations eventually.

6. When we're ministering to messy people, it is inevitable that the mess will eventually spill onto us.

   Share with your group a time when you were helping someone, and their mess spilled over on you.

   6a. Was it "bearing" or "forgiveness" that was required?

7. What's the difference between the call to bear with someone and the call to forgive them?

   7a. How do you know when either one is needed?

## Digging into the Word

1.  Read John 13:1–17.
    1a. Describe the significance of "his hour."

3.  Describe the act of servanthood that Christ engaged in at this supper (vv. 4–12).

4.  In this pivotal moment in his ministry, did Jesus choose to show his love primarily through words or actions?

5.  What does this act say about the type of caregiving we should be giving as Christ's servants (v. 14)?

6.  Jesus' kingdom is an upside-down kingdom. Contrast the world's pattern of approaching messy people with Christ's pattern.

| World | Christ |
|---|---|
| Boundaries | |
| Formal setting | |
| Appointments | |
| Limited involvement | |

## For Additional Study

John tells us that Jesus is the Word. "In the beginning was the Word, and the Word was with God, and the Word was God." Look up the following passages and describe some of the things the Word *does*, noting the practical significance of the act for the recipient.

| Verse | What the Word Does | Practical Significance |
|---|---|---|
| John 2:1–11 | | |
| Luke 5:1–11 | | |
| Mark 1:30–31 | | |
| Mark 1:40–45 | | |
| Matt. 8:5–13 | | |
| Luke 7:11–18 | | |
| Matt. 8:23–27 | | |
| Matt. 8:28–34 | | |
| Luke 8:43–48 | | |
| Matt. 14:15–21 | | |
| John 11:1–46 | | |
| John 21:25 | | |

## Putting It Into Practice—Homework

Sometimes, we can read a story about how a Christian ministers to someone else in a practical way and think, "Wow, I could do that...but I just never have the opportunity." There are certainly several reasons out of your control why you may not have had the opportunity to serve in a similar way. But, there are at least two reasons that may prevent many opportunities to serve that *are* within your control:

○ Shallow relationships
○ Busyness

Much of this study has covered ways to deepen your relationships. Included in the lessons are ideas like listening well, loving deeply, and seeking to know others. As you probably already know, these kinds of relationships take a great investment of time. Sometimes we miss the needs of others because our schedules are packed so tight with appointments, events, and meetings we simply don't have the opportunity to see the needs around us.

## Application

How do you organize your time? Do you use a planner, online calendar, or wall calendar? Or do you barely use a calendar at all? Whatever it is that you use, spend some time looking at the month ahead. Consider the following questions:

○ What days tend to be busiest?
○ What days typically have more free time?
○ How do you usually spend your weekends?
○ What fills your evenings?

Philippians 2:4 says, "Let each of you look not only to his own interests, but also to the interests of others." Does your schedule reflect your willingness to look to the interests of others?

It's inevitable that some of us will have more flexibility than others. But, regardless of our life situation, genuine love compels us to schedule our time in such a way that we maintain flexibility for ministering to one another. If you're unable to carve out time to be available to serve others, perhaps ask yourself what is driving your priorities.

In addition, different types of service will take up different amounts of time. A task like cooking a meal for a neighbor may take an hour or two, while sending a text to a friend you haven't heard from in awhile will take a very small amount of time.

Take stock of how you spend your time. Pray and ask God to help you order your time for his glory. Use the chart below to consider how you might plan to serve others throughout your week. What types of things on your schedule could you do with someone else? Can you invite a friend to your child's weekly soccer practice to catch up with them? Can you schedule one night a week to invite someone in your church over for dinner? Could you structure an extra hour to mow your elderly neighbor's lawn a few Saturdays a month? What days can you schedule "flex" time that is kept available to serve others as needs arise?

| | |
|---|---|
| Sunday | |
| Monday | |
| Tuesday | |
| Wednesday | |
| Thursday | |
| Friday | |
| Saturday | |

Although it might seem tedious, it can be helpful to actively schedule this flexible time into your week. As you practice the habit of being available to minister to others, you'll begin to make that time available more naturally. If you find yourself having difficulty finding time to minister, refer back to the "Digging into the Word" portion of this chapter. Study Christ's character and his willingness to serve others.

In addition to the individual you have been ministering to throughout this study, who else has God placed in your life that you ought to be pursuing? How do those relationships fit into your realistic schedule?

## PRAYER PROMPTS

This week, consider the following as you pray for your friend.

○ Ask God to help you see your time as ultimately his, rather than as your own.

○ Pray that you'd be motivated by Christ's sacrificial love to open your schedule to ministry.

○ Pray that you would consider service to those around you, even in the midst of your set appointments and responsibilities.

○ Pray that you would grow in Christlikeness and selflessness as you minister to your friend.

○ Pray that you would grow in trust that the Lord will sustain your energy as you offer your time to his purposes.

# 4

## How Do We Truthfully Speak?

# SPEAKING TO ONE ANOTHER

- ○ *While serving one another is essential, we cannot truly minister to others without using our words to apply the truth of Scripture to hearts that desperately need it.*

- ○ *Sometimes, seeking to affirm may be all that is needed to produce Christian growth in the life of a believer.*

- ○ *Other times, biblically rooted correction will be required.*

- ○ *In every situation, we can be sure that those we are ministering to will always need to be given hope.*

## STORY

### SHANNON McCOY

I met Mindy soon after her 50th birthday. She had recently celebrated the big occasion with all of her friends and family as they gathered in her beautifully manicured backyard to honor her. Mindy said that the entire evening was magical.

Days later she was shrouded in a dark cloud and unable to get out of bed. Her husband thought she had come down with a virus, but she wasn't physically sick. Mindy was despondent. She didn't know how she got there and was disturbed by the darkness that enveloped her. What was happening concerned both Mindy and her husband.

A mutual friend from church told Mindy she might want to talk to me. Our friend knew I was familiar with darkness and depression and might be able to help. Mindy called and we set up an afternoon together to talk through what was going on.

It took everything Mindy had to get out of bed and drag herself to my house that day. Mindy told me that she lacked all desire or motivation. She said she typically wasn't like that at all.

87

Mindy prided herself as someone who had always been driven to succeed.

As I asked deeper questions, I perceived that Mindy craved attention and intimacy. She believed the way to get it was to succeed and to be the best at everything. Mindy often felt invisible and not valued as she was growing up. She learned to be an over-achiever. She participated in sports, science fairs, and academic contests. She got first place in almost everything she did. Mindy enjoyed receiving accolades from her teachers and peers.

I asked Mindy to tell me what happened if she felt like she failed. She said it was more about not getting attention. Success brought with it a certain satisfaction for her desire to be seen. Mindy said she fought to not feel invisible, including invisible to God.

Mindy and I sat silent for a few minutes. I could tell she probably had doubts about God, especially about his goodness and his love. I asked where she thought those feelings might have come from.

Mindy said she grew up in a household full of verbal, emotional, and physical abuse. On many occasions, she said, her father yelled and screamed at her mother for hours on end. Sometimes her dad would even hit her mom, which sent Mindy's older brother into a rage to try to get in the middle and stop the fighting. Mindy would cower behind the couch out of fear, her younger sister would cry uncontrollably, and both would pray their dad wouldn't take out his rage on either of them.

When the fighting was over, Mindy acted as the peacemaker. She would be the one to clean up the mess. Mindy would try unsuccessfully to console her mother or brother, or try to stop her sister from crying. She especially longed to please her father. But the only time she got his attention was when she had a major accomplishment. Mindy remembered during one of her dad's tirades against her mom she tried to get her dad's attention by showing him the first-place award she got in a contest. He noticed, but not for very long before he was back to screaming at her mom.

Mindy admitted it was difficult for her to translate her experience with her earthly father into a trust for her heavenly Father. But she admitted she was weary of trying to get satisfaction from the attention of others and never being satisfied. She was tired of seeking the intimacy she craved, and becoming angry and bitter when she didn't get it.

Mindy looked at me with tears in her eyes and softly sobbed. She said she was desperate to find an answer to her problem.

I didn't know exactly what to say. I knew God's Word had wisdom for all the suffering we endure in this world, but I wasn't sure what would be the most hopeful and helpful in that particular moment for Mindy. I thought about one of the passages the Lord had ministered to me in my own despondency. Psalm 73 was one of my "go to" passages for times of trouble. So, I took a chance and asked if she would be okay if I read it out loud. Thankfully, she said yes.

I swiped my phone and started reading while simultaneously asking the Lord to minister his words to her soul. "Truly God is good to Israel, to those who are pure in heart . . . "

When I was done reading, Mindy said she could identify with how Asaph felt hopeless and unsatisfied with his life and allowed his negative feelings to control him. She said she heard his desperation until he turned his focus on God alone.

Mindy asked me to read the part when Asaph asked whom he had in heaven. There was something she wanted to hear again.

"Whom have I in heaven but you," I read, "And there is nothing on earth that I desire besides you. But for me it is good to be near God; I have made the Lord GOD my refuge, that I may tell of all your works."

Mindy sighed deeply when I finished reading. "I remember thinking that the couch I was hiding behind was a sort of refuge. I can see now that it was the Lord all along who protected me," Mindy said. "I guess I never really thought about God being near during those awful times," she continued, "and that he, the invisible one, was always present to care for me."

As Mindy got her things together to leave, I silently thanked God. I could tell from how Mindy responded to his word that she had learned her only hope for a satisfied heart was in God alone. Mindy thanked me for taking a chance and sharing the passages. She said she had gained a new perspective and a right view of God and herself from God's words through Asaph. I knew we had many more conversations ahead of us. But I encouraged Mindy to continue considering what it would mean to exchange an earthly perspective of her life for an eternal perspective, and we committed to meet again.

## GROUP DISCUSSION AND REFLECTION

1.  The group in the video mentioned the following verses for giving hope to "messy" people. Look up each verse. How does the truth in each one of these passages give you hope?

    1a.  Psalm 9:9–10

    1b.  Psalm 5:3, 11

    1c.  Matthew 11:28–30

    1d.  1 Peter 1:6–7

1e.  Galatians 2:20

2.  What are some of the places in Scripture you go to most often to help give others hope?

*Share these with your group and explain why they are useful.*

3.  Does biblical affirmation come naturally to you, or do you tend to find it more difficult?

4.  How have you seen those you minister to blessed by your use of biblical affirmation? Discuss together as a group.

5.  Does biblical correction come naturally to you, or do you tend to find it more difficult?

6. How have you seen those you minister to blessed by your use of biblical correction?

*Discuss together as a group.*

7. Of the four ways of "truthing in love" (giving hope, affirming, correcting, teaching) which of them do you need to improve in the most?

8. How can you practically strive to grow in this area?

9. Write down some of the ways that other members in your group intend to improve. Chances are, we will all need to grow in similar ways as we strive to provide gospel care.

## DIGGING INTO THE WORD

1.  Read Hebrews 3:12–15.
2.  What is the main characteristic of an evil heart in verse 12?

2a. How should this shape your loving confrontation toward those living in a mess?

3.  What does biblical exhortation entail (v. 13)?
    (See also Heb. 10:24–25; 1 Thess. 5:14.)

3a. What does it mean to "share in Christ?"

4. Write down some of the ways you've been encouraged (through God's Word) to have confidence in God.

5. In between seeking God in prayer and waiting to hear God's answer (Ps. 5:3; Heb. 3:15), what should people stuck in a mess do so that their hearts will not harden? How can you help them? (Heb. 3:12)

## For Additional Study

In the general session, Scott quoted Wayne Mack saying, "Hope is a biblically based expectation of good." Therefore, hope indicates that:

- ○ God is real;
- ○ Transformation is possible;
- ○ The best is yet to come.

What passages in the Bible substantiate these characteristics of hope?

## Putting It Into Practice—Homework

Many times, people find it intimidating to provide gospel care because they don't know what to say. But anyone who has spent any length of time ministering to others has probably discovered this secret: you don't need to figure out the perfect words to say from within yourself. The words you need are all right there in the Bible.

The Lord has provided words that are much more comforting, timely, appropriate, and piercing than any we could come up with ourselves. Studying the Bible helps us to know God's words—to "bind them on [our] fingers [and] write them on the tablet of [our] hearts" (Prov. 7:3).

So, as you minister to others, it's important to be growing in your understanding of God and his Word. Some people do this by reading and meditating, and others use memorization as well. Some use artwork to dwell on God's Word, and some study the passage as if preparing to teach it. Pick one of the following Scriptures to interact with, whether by memorizing it or using another method.

- ○ Psalm 9:9–10
- ○ Psalm 5:3, 11
- ○ Matthew 11:28–30
- ○ 1 Peter 1:6–7
- ○ Galatians 2:20

As you interact with this Scripture, be sure to read the surrounding passage to grasp its context. Consider how you might use the passage you selected to minister to another person. Try a few of the following ideas to interact with the passage:

1. Study the passage, as if preparing to teach it.

2. Memorize the passage.

3. Create a piece of artwork, using the passage as inspiration.

4. Read the passage out loud repeatedly, multiple times a day.

5. Set the passage to music, or find a hymn that reflects the truths of the passage so that you may sing it.

## APPLICATION

1. In what types of situations might you apply this passage of Scripture? Would you offer it to a person who is without hope? Fearful? Overcome with joy? Walking in sin? What would you say about the passage?

2. How does this passage apply to your life specifically? Is there any connection in your life that you might be able to share as you minister with this passage to another person?

3. What about the specific person you've been ministering to? How could you share this passage with them in a loving way? Are they in need of correction, hope, affirmation, or teaching? Could this passage be what is most needed for them?

4. Use this guide from Hebrews 10:23–25 to write an exhortation specific to your friend. Be sure to share it with them next time you meet.

> *Let us hold fast the confession of our hope without wavering, for he who promised is faithful. And let us consider how to stir up one another to love and good works, not neglecting to meet together, as is the habit of some, but encouraging one another, and all the more as you see the Day drawing near.*

CONFESSION OF HOPE

1. What is the hope that your friend has in Christ? Remind them of the gospel.

*STIR UP TO LOVE AND GOOD WORKS*

2.  Is your friend neglecting to love and serve? How can you help motivate them?

3.  Are they serving others well? Encourage them by sharing with them how you've seen them serve and love others.

*NOT NEGLECTING TO MEET*

4.  What does "community" look like for your friend? Are they keeping in contact with the family of God, including you? What might you say to encourage them to continue meeting with people?

*ENCOURAGE ONE ANOTHER*

5.  How have you seen your friend grow in the Lord through this process? How have you learned more about God through them? Share that with them.

6.  Is your friend walking in sin that needs to be corrected? What can you say to them to encourage them to repent?

7.  Is your friend seeking wisdom? What wisdom do you have from Scripture to help teach them?

## Prayer Prompts

This week, pray for the following things as you minister:

- Pray that the Lord would strengthen you to use your words in a way that glorifies him.

- Pray that your time spent in Bible reading would strengthen your love for God as well as your love for your friend.

- Pray that the Lord would grant you wisdom as you consider whether your friend might need correction, hope, affirmation, or teaching.

- Pray that your exhortation would be encouraging and edifying to your friend.

- Pray that you would share your exhortation with your friend in love.

# 5

What Does a Life that Consistently Applies the Gospel Look Like (Gospeling)?

# GOSPELING ONE ANOTHER (PART 1)

- *If you patiently listen to someone, serve them, and speak truth into their life, chances are they are going to change.*

- *They will probably feel better, think better thoughts, and may even change their behavior. However, without the application of the gospel to hearts, only surface-level change can be achieved.*

- *Without the gospel, the change that takes place is not biblical transformation.*

- *Without the gospel, the change that takes place loses its true lasting power.*

- *We need to begin by identifying the need of gospel truth in the face of both the external source of our problems (suffering) and the internal source of our problems (sin).*

## STORY

### FAWN KEMBLE

I hadn't seen her in a while, so I called just to check in and she asked if she could come over. Her voice sounded flat. After brewing tea, I sat next to her on the couch and asked how she was doing.

"I'm okay. Just feeling a little sad, that's all. Nothing big. Just felt like maybe I should talk to someone before I get depressed, you know?"

She'd struggled with depression in her past and God had brought her through it, so this made sense. When I asked if there was anything in particular making her feel sad, she said, "Not really, nothing terrible happened or anything."

After sitting with her, sipping tea, and catching up on some of the day-to-day stuff of life, it came out that her roommate was getting married. "I'm so happy for her!" she said, her smile genuine. "He's such a good guy, and they're going to be great together." At this point, her smile faltered and she sighed. "I guess I'm going to have to start looking for a new roommate, or move again."

I could see that this was bringing out some of her sadness, as tears threatened to fall. She held them back, trying so hard to be stoic. I asked if that was hard for her.

"It's just that we get along so well. She's the best roommate I ever had, and I've had a lot of them. And I can't afford to live alone. But it's okay, I mean, I'm so thrilled for her and it's not that big of a deal. I've just had to do this a lot. I guess I'm just a bit tired. But I'm fine! I don't want you to think I'm jealous or bitter or anything! I'm fine. Compared to many others, my life is really good."

At this point she put her head in her hands and tried to cover up the beginnings of a few tears. I offered her a tissue, and she looked up with a sad smile and said, "I don't know what's wrong with me. I have a good life! I don't want to be ungrateful to God. I've got a great job, I love our church, my friends and family are doing well. I have nothing to be sad about, really. It's just that I've been through this for two decades, now, and when I look ahead to the future, all I can see is single me, finding a roommate, becoming close, them getting engaged, me having to move again and again and again. Everyone else around me seems to find a more permanent partner, to move forward in life, get married, have kids, and I'm just here, always in the same position. I'm just tired. And sad. But I know I shouldn't be."

At this point, I could see my dear friend was genuinely suffering what many of us who are single into our forties suffer, but she wasn't allowing herself to recognize it for what it was. She was downplaying it, trying to be strong, positive, grateful. What she really needed to do at this moment was recognize her pain and lament to her Heavenly Father.

I wrapped her up in my arms and told her I was so sorry she was suffering in this way, that what she was describing sounded exhausting and heartbreaking, and that she didn't need to be fine. It was okay for her to be broken about this, to feel sad. I reminded her that her desire for a more permanent home, a more permanent partner in life, was a good desire and that God saw that desire—his heart aching with hers in her sadness. I reminded her that 1 Peter 5:7 tells us to cast all our anxieties on him because he cares for us! She wasn't ungrateful for feeling loss. God wanted her to pour out her heart to him, and let him walk through her sadness with her. I told her that Jesus himself was "a man of sorrows, acquainted with grief," so he understood. At this point, she finally let herself weep over this grief for the first time.

We sat on that couch, weeping together as our tea got cold. There would be other conversations to come, plans to be made in the future about roommates and apartments and trusting God with her life. But that afternoon, she needed comfort. She needed reassurance from a friend that her heartbreaks mattered to God. She needed to be told she didn't always have to be strong. She needed to run into her Father's arms and let him hold her, and to have a friend hold her and weep with her just as Romans 12 says. She needed to admit that her suffering was real, and to lament before God.

In this moment, the best way I could love this friend was not to jump right into the practicalities, give her false promises that God has "the one" out there and all she needs to do is wait, or chastise her for feeling sad. The best way to love her was to acknowledge that her suffering was real and mattered to me and to God, and teach her how to lament. Psalm 62:8 says "Trust in him at all times, O people; pour out your heart before him; God is a refuge for us." Sometimes, the best first step is to help our friends pour out their hearts before God and take refuge in him.

## GROUP DISCUSSION AND REFLECTION

### GOSPELING AND SUFFERING

1. How have you seen people downplay suffering in their lives?

2. What does it look like for you to invite someone to biblically lament?

3. Look up the following Psalms on lament. Talk about whether they are best to pray personally or corporately.

   ○ Psalm 3
   ○ Psalm 12
   ○ Psalm 44
   ○ Psalm 59
   ○ Psalm 60
   ○ Psalm 71
   ○ Psalm 80
   ○ Psalm 94
   ○ Psalm 120

*GOSPELING AND SIN*

4.  How have you seen people downplay the depth of sin in their lives?

5.  What does it look like for you to invite someone to biblically confess something?

6.  Discuss these passages. How would you teach someone about confession?
    ○   Psalm 32:5
    ○   James 5:16
    ○   1 John 1:5–1

7.  How have you seen your personal ministry to others fall short when you have failed to help them understand the depth of their mess (in either suffering or sin)?

*Share one of your experiences with the group.*

## DIGGING INTO THE WORD

1. Read 1 Corinthians 15:1–5.
2. What does Paul identify as each of the following:

   2a. Our problem

---

   2b. God's solution

---

   2c. Our response

---

3. In these passages, how does the gospel continue to progressively work?

---

4. What's the significance of the phrase "in accordance with the Scriptures"?

---

# For Additional Study

1. On a sheet of paper, create two columns. On one side, explain how you would share the gospel with someone who is struggling under the weight of sin. On the other side, explain how you would provide hope through the gospel for someone who is struggling under the weight of suffering.

    1a. What is the same?

    1b. Where are the differences in emphasis?

## PUTTING IT INTO PRACTICE—HOMEWORK

### BIBLICAL LAMENT

God created us as individuals who learn by example. Paul notes this in his first letter to the Corinthians, writing, "Imitate me, just as I imitate Christ" (1 Cor. 11:1). It is helpful to have someone to watch and imitate as we learn something new. For many Christians, the idea of lament is brand new. Many of us were taught to honor God by keeping quiet, rather than by bringing our cares to him. Thankfully, we have several examples to follow in Scripture. In fact, the book of Lamentations is a full collection of laments from Jeremiah. As we begin to grasp the biblical discipline of lament, pay close attention to the examples the Lord has provided to us in his Word.

### EXAMPLES OF BIBLICAL LAMENT
- Lamentations 3
- Psalm 42
- Psalm 102
- Psalm 13

### PRACTICE

Another learning tool is practice. As Paul writes in his letter to the Philippians, "What you have . . . seen in me, practice these things" (Phil. 4:9). After you've considered the example of biblical lament, spend some time crafting your own biblical lament (in the form of a written prayer to God). Your lament does not need to be intricate or elaborate. Simply focus on being honest, maintaining a reverence and understanding for God. Use Lamentations 3:21–24 or Psalm 42 as your guide, along with the following questions.

- What about life in a sin-cursed world is causing you pain, anguish, or disappointment right now?

- How does it make you feel that you're experiencing these things right now? Are you sad? Disappointed? Angry? Hurt? Do you feel betrayed? Lonely? Forgotten?

- What are some truths you know about God and his character?

- What do the Lord's unchanging characteristics mean for your circumstances?

## MODEL

Our personal growth and sanctification are never meant to end with us. The Lord offers each of us comfort "so that we may be able to comfort those who are in any affliction, with the comfort with which we ourselves are comforted by God" (2 Cor. 1:4). Has the Lord comforted you through learning about biblical lament? Share that comfort with the friend you have been ministering to. Model biblical lament to your friend, highlighting your suffering and the character of God to them. Help your friend craft their own biblical lament, crying to God for his comfort and nearness.

## BIBLICAL CONFESSION

Although God tells us directly "if we confess our sins, he is faithful and just to forgive us our sins" (1 John 1:9), confession of sin is so often a discipline that Christians neglect. It can be difficult to look our own sin in the face and understand its depth. It is easy to feel like we are hiding our sins; most people around us do not know the specifics of our sin. We're able to put on a façade, convincing those around us that we have everything together or, at the very least, we're not as bad as "that guy."

Jesus told a parable about a person who seemed to have this problem with confession. In his story, a Pharisee loudly proclaimed his supposed righteousness before the temple, noting that he was not as bad as the tax collector near him (Luke 18:11). In great contrast, the tax collector cries out, "God, be merciful to me, a sinner!" (Luke 18:13). The tax collector's confession, Christ says, brought justification, while the Pharisee's did not.

It can be difficult to face our own sin, to see the brokenness of our own hearts, and to see its consequences. But, in that difficult place, on our knees in humble confession is exactly where we find forgiveness. God promises us that.

Using the same dynamic of imitation, practicing, and modeling, work through an understanding of biblical confession. Pay attention to the examples of confession God has provided for us in his Word.

## Examples of Confession

- 1 Samuel 15:24
- 2 Samuel 2:13
- Psalm 32
- Psalm 51
- Luke 5:8
- Luke 15:18–19

## Practice

Although it may feel forced to practice confession so mechanically, practicing it continually will help you form it into a God-glorifying habit. Craft your own confession of sin (in the form of a written prayer to God), using either Psalm 32 or 51 as a guide, along with the following questions.

- Against whom have you sinned? In what way did you sin? How did your sin affect others? How did it affect you?

- What does the Bible say about those who confess sin? What hope do sinners have?

- What are the truths you know about God and his character? What do these mean for your sin?

- How can you work to turn from this sin? What can motivate you to put off this sin and put on righteousness?

## Model

The apostle John writes, "If we walk in the light, as he is in the light, we have fellowship with one another, and the blood of Jesus his son cleanses us from all sin" (1 John 1:7). God asks us to confess our sins not because he is unaware of them, but because confession opens the door for forgiveness and grace. Not only that, he also uses confession as a way to strengthen Christian fellowship. As you share your confession of sin with your friend, you are inviting them to walk in deeper fellowship with both you and God. Communicate with your friend about the forgiveness Christians can receive as they confess their sins. Invite your friend to confess their own sins, helping them to understand the depth of grace they have received.

## Prayer Prompts

This week, use the following list to guide your prayers.

- Confess your sins to God and ask for his forgiveness.
- Thank God for his gift of forgiveness, mercy, fellowship, and light.
- Pray that your friend would be edified, both by your lament and your confession that you share with them.
- Pray that you'd understand the importance of biblical lament and confession, and incorporate them into your own life.
- Pray that your friend would find the freedom and hope that comes from humble confession of sin.

# Session 8

## Gospeling One Another (Part 2)

- *When you help someone see the suffering and self-worship that are contributing to their mess, they will realize that the problem is worse than they ever thought.*

- *But that just means that God's redemption, grace, and mercy is greater than they ever imagined.*

- *After recognizing suffering and identifying self-worship, we then must confidently remind one another of gospel truth, because it is through the regular and consistent reminders of the gospel (and all of its implications) that our hearts are inspired to worship God and true transformation takes place.*

- *In light of this reminder, we also must call one another to live a life in step with the gospel, helping them to identify the practical ways God is calling them to change and live out their freedom in Christ through radical obedience.*

## Story

### Rachel Cain

My friend Catherine and I got married on the same weekend, four years ago, before we knew each other. Catherine was six years older than me and began having babies right away. By the time we met, she was eight months pregnant with her first child and only two years into marriage. She and her husband came from opposite upbringings. Catherine was born in the country, while Daniel was born in the city. Catherine was a straight-A student, while Daniel had a criminal record. Catherine was discipled into the faith by her family, while Daniel didn't learn of Christ until adulthood.

All these differences aside, they loved each other and loved the Lord. However, their marriage was one that took a lot of work. While there was no cause for concern about domestic abuse, Catherine and Daniel bickered about everything. They endured conflict after conflict. Usually, they had arguments over small matters, but their arguments turned heated, with raised voices and hurtful words. In addition to frequent arguments, they had financial pressure, stressful jobs, and a brand-new baby. Catherine sought guidance and wisdom from me and invited me into the "mess" of her marriage. She desperately wanted help. In my eagerness to help, I spent hours listening to her pore over the details of each argument. Catherine recited to me both the words she said and the words Daniel said. She analyzed her thoughts and feelings with me, wondering how broken her marriage was and wondering if she'd ever have hope to fix it.

So, we met weekly. If there's anything I did well as I met with Catherine, it was listening. I listened to her for hours. And I felt so much compassion for her struggles. I felt I had a really good handle on what it was like in her marriage day to day. Our meetings would begin with prayer, then she would begin telling me about her week. She'd give me an overview of each of their arguments that week, along with her personal analysis on the problem. I listened closely and tried my best to offer biblical wisdom that might help her work through the issues.

One day, she was asking about budgeting. They'd gotten in an argument about money, particularly as it applied to Daniel's hobbies. I'd recently read a book about a biblical perspective on finances, so I offered her all the knowledge I had. I encouraged her to be generous with her money, to seek her husband's interests over her own, and to trust the Lord with her finances. Our meetings went on like this for a few months. She'd note her problem of the week, and I'd offer her a three-step plan to get over that problem, with Bible verses included. I thought I'd been doing a great job as a counselor!

At some point, due to the prompting of the Holy Spirit I am sure, I began to wonder why Catherine and Daniel were still arguing so often about such trivial matters. Why wasn't my practical, biblical advice helping them avoid conflict? As I prepared for our next meeting that week, I realized what I had been missing. I had offered Catherine plenty of practical advice, but I had withheld from her the *true* help that remembering the gospel provides.

Sitting across from Catherine that week, I felt silly. I sought her forgiveness and outlined where I thought I'd gotten off base. And as we sat, we discussed the truths of the gospel for the first time in our friendship. We considered the implications of the gospel story on each of our lives. I had assumed that we both could move on from the basics of the gospel, since we were both longtime believers. Surely, we both understood the gospel by now! But as we closed in prayer, we both felt refreshed.

We did this for a month or more—coming together to consider the wonders of Christ and his great love for us. Of course, she and her husband still ran into conflicts, and she still sought my advice. But instead of trying to use my spiritual tips and tricks to overcome it, she was using the power of the Holy Spirit and the truth of the gospel. Through Christ's sacrifice, she found strength to sacrifice for her marriage. By God's grace, she was able to offer grace to her husband. True transformation began to happen as the gospel took deeper and deeper root in her heart.

## Group Discussion and Reflection

1. Why is it important for believers to be reminded of the gospel?

*Share a time when someone reminded you of the truth of the gospel and how it impacted you.*

2. How have you seen the gospel take deeper root in people's lives in a way that produces genuine spiritual transformation? Share with your group the following:

    2a. When you helped someone see the gospel afresh in the midst of their sin.

    2b. When you helped someone see the gospel afresh in the midst of their suffering.

2c. What are some of the implications of the gospel that people regularly need to be reminded of? Identify specific passages of Scripture that teach these implications.

2d. What does it look like to instruct others in gospel commands? What specific passages might you use to identify specific commands?

2e. What can you do to help make those commands practical?

2f. What does it look like to remind others of God's goodness? What specific passages might you use to identify specific truths?

2g. What can you do to help people see and appreciate God's goodness?

3. Write down some of what other members in your group share about God's goodness and his commands.

4. Why is it impossible to trust God and obey him without remembering the truth of the gospel first?

## Digging into the Word

1. Read Psalm 111.
2. Write down what these passages tell us about God.

| | |
|---|---|
| 111:2 | *For example: His works are great* |
| 111:3 | |
| 111:3 | |
| 111:4 | |
| 111:4 | |
| 111:5 | |
| 111:5 | |
| 111:6 | |
| 111:6 | |
| 111:7 | |
| 111:7 | |
| 111:8 | |
| 111:8 | |
| 111:9 | |
| 111:9 | |
| 111:9 | |
| 111:10 | |

A.W. Tozer, in his book *The Knowledge of the Holy*, writes, "A right conception of God is basic not only to theology, but to practical Christian living as well."[2] Using the information you found for the chart above, write out how the particular knowledge of God ought to shape how you live your life.

| | |
|---|---|
| 111:2 | *For Example: If God's works differ from mine, and his are good, I can trust his plan for my life.* |
| 111:3 | |
| 111:3 | |
| 111:4 | |
| 111:4 | |
| 111:5 | |
| 111:5 | |
| 111:6 | |
| 111:6 | |
| 111:7 | |
| 111:7 | |
| 111:8 | |
| 111:8 | |
| 111:9 | |
| 111:9 | |
| 111:9 | |
| 111:10 | |

## Putting It Into Practice—Homework

Much of the time, Christians talk about the importance of speaking the gospel in reference to evangelism. For many people, it seems as if the gospel is helpful for initial salvation, but not for the process of progressive sanctification. But that was not the Lord's plan for the gospel story at all. From eternity past, the Lord purposed his gospel narrative to be not only for the salvation of believers but also an important reminder for our ongoing journey of becoming more like him.

## Application

1. How have you been reminded of the gospel, especially in difficult times? If you aren't sure, think about the following difficult circumstances you may have experienced:
   - Loneliness
   - Fear
   - Uncertainty about the future
   - The need to make an important decision
   - Hopelessness
   - Disappointment
   - Conflict in relationships
   - Sickness

2. Choose one of the circumstances above that you've experienced. Take some time to think through how you applied (or should have applied) the gospel to your life in these circumstances. Write out some of your thoughts in preparation to share this with your friend.

3. The gospel is just as practical in positive times as it is in negative times. It is a common mistake to run to God in the difficulties, yet forget the glory and necessity of the gospel even in the good times. How can we remind ourselves and others of the gospel in the following positive circumstances?

- ○ Joy
- ○ Relaxation
- ○ Comfort
- ○ Excitement about the future
- ○ Healthy relationships
- ○ Enjoyment of hobbies
- ○ Peace

4. Choose one of the circumstances above that you've experienced. Take some time to think through how you applied (or should have applied) the gospel to your life in these circumstances. Write out some of your thoughts in preparation to share this with your friend.

5. Now, consider what your friend is facing. Are they still experiencing hardship? Have they entered into a more positive season? In what ways can you practically remind your friend of the gospel in the circumstances they are experiencing now? In what ways is God calling them to a

renewed trust or obedience in response to the truth of the gospel?

6. Use the chart below to practice applying the gospel to these situations.

| What does the gospel mean for...? | An applicable gospel truth | An applicable character trait of God | An act of trust or obedience motivated by love for God |
|---|---|---|---|
| Joy: | God has offered me undeserved grace | God is good | Share my joy by rejoicing with others |
| Loneliness: | God has invited me into relationship with him | God is ever present | Seek satisfaction in God by ministering to others |
| Other: | | | |
| Other: | | | |
| Other: | | | |

As you remind your friend of the gospel, ask them to remind *you* of the gospel! Whether you are experiencing hard times or pleasant times, ask them to remind you of the gospel throughout the week, and how God is calling you to respond in trust and obedience.

Additionally, ask them to choose one of their other friends to begin serving and ministering to as well. Offer to help them walk through the logistics of ministering to someone. Pray with your friend for the person they will seek to minister to.

## Prayer Prompts

- ○ Pray that your friend would find someone to minister to practically.
- ○ Pray that your friend would grow in sanctification as they minister.
- ○ Pray that you would be motivated by God's love to continue to minister to others.
- ○ Pray that you would seek hope and comfort from the gospel, rather than worldly comforts.

# 6

## Answer Guide

# Answer Guide

## The Calling of All Christians

### Digging into the Word

1. Read Ephesians 4:7–16.

2. Identify all of the gifts listed in these passages.

| | |
|---|---|
| 4:7 | Grace (according to Christ's gift) |
| 4:8 | Gifts (see Psalm 68:18) |
| 4:11 | Apostles |
| 4:11 | Prophets |
| 4:11 | Evangelists |
| 4:11 | Shepherds |
| 4:11 | Teachers |
| 4:13 | Unity |
| 4:13 | Knowledge of the Son |
| 4:13 | Maturity |
| 4:13 | Stature of the fullness Christ |
| 4:14 | Maturity |
| 4:15 | Maturity |
| 4:16 | Unity, growth, love |

3. Why were the "office" gifts given to the church (4:12)?
   *To equip the saints*

3a. How do you view the responsibility of the "officers" of the church?
   (Answers vary)

4. Whom has God called to do the "work of ministry" in the church (pastors or all the "saints")? How should this shape our expectations for the church family?

    *The equipping that our leaders provide should lead to action in building up the church, discipleship, and caring for the body.*

4a. Did you know that God calls YOU to build his church?

    (Answers vary)

4b. What do you think that looks like practically in your life?

    (Answers vary)

5. What is the ultimate goal the ministry of the "saints" is working toward (see gifts above)?

    *Unity of faith, maturity, knowledge of the Son, to resemble our Elder Brother, Christ*

6. What are some of the waves that toss people and carry them away from knowing and believing the truth?

    (Answers vary)

7. What are the practical ways we (the "saints") can encourage our struggling brothers and sisters when they are tossed to and fro (4:14–15)?

    *Speak truth*

    *Teach good doctrine*

    *Remind them of the truth found in the Word*

    *Graciously guide them back on the paths of life*

8. What happens when the whole body works in unity, bonded together by the gracious gifts of God?

    *The body of Christ grows*

## FOR ADDITIONAL STUDY

1. Identify the spiritual blessings in Ephesians 1–3 that equip the saints for the work of ministry.

   (See Appendix 1)

2. Identify the blessings God gives his people in Psalm 68. Paul references these gifts when he encourages the church in Ephesus.

   (See Appendix 2)

# THE ART OF GOSPEL CARE

## DIGGING INTO THE WORD

1. Read Philippians 1:1–17

2. How did Paul feel about the church in Philippi?

   *Thankful*

   *He considered them "with joy"*

   *Partners in the work of the gospel*

   *Confident in their sanctification*

   *Brothers and sisters in Christ*

   *With the affection of Jesus*

2a. When you think about your immediate family, church family, and friends, what are some thoughts and feelings that come to mind?

   *Answers vary*

3. What did Paul hope for this church?

   *Love may abound more and more, with knowledge and all discernment*

   *Approve what is excellent*

   *Be pure and blameless for the day of Christ*

   *Be filled with the fruit of righteousness that comes through Jesus Christ, to the glory and praise of God*

4. What did Paul say advanced the gospel?

   *His imprisonment*

4a. We often make plans when we think about caring for a friend in a messy situation—for example, what we might say or how we need to approach them. What character trait does God tend to use in these relationships, rather than a simple "script"?

   *Our humility*

5. How did the gospel inform Paul's words?

   *It made him speak to them with boldness*

6. What is the right way to "preach the gospel" (according to this passage)?

   *Out of love*

   *Knowing that we are put there for the defense of **the gospel** (not a defense of self)*

7. What is the wrong way (according to this passage)?

   *Proclaim Christ out of selfish ambition, not sincerely but to inflict pain*

## For Additional Study

1. Read Philippians 2:1–8, 12

2. Make a list of all the instructions Paul lists for how to approach one another in care.

| Verse | Action |
|---|---|
| 1 | Pursue encouragement in Christ |
| 1 | Acknowledge comfort from love |
| 1 | Participate in conflict by the power of the Spirit |
| 1 | Show affection and sympathy for others |
| 2 | Complete Paul's joy by being of the same mind, |
| 2 | and having the same love |
| 2 | Be in full accord (see also Eph. 4:4–6) |

Continued . . .

| Verse | Action |
|---|---|
| 3 | Do nothing from selfish ambition |
| 3 | Do nothing from conceit |
| 3 | Have a humble spirit |
| 3 | Count others more significant than yourself |
| 4 | Look beyond your own interests (put off) |
| 4 | Look to the interests of others (put on) |
| 5 | Have the mind of Christ |
| 6 | Don't play God |
| 7, 8 | Be a humble servant in the hands of God |
| 12 | Work out your own salvation with fear and trembling |

# THE CENTRALITY OF LOVE

## DIGGING INTO THE WORD

1. Read 1 John 4:7–5:2

2. Why does John say we should love one another?

   *Because of God and his love for us (v. 7, 11)*

3. What are the implications if someone does not exhibit love toward their neighbor?

   *It shows we do not truly know God (v. 8)*

4. What is love?

   *God loved us and sent his Son to reconcile us to him (v. 10)*

5. What sustains your love of others?

   *"By this we know that we love the children of God, when we love God" (5:2).*

6. How does genuine love manifest in our emotions? In our thoughts? In our actions?

   (Answers vary)

7. How does John tell us that people will see the evidence of the Holy Spirit in our lives?

    *When we love one another (v. 12–13)*

7a. Anyone can love. What makes the Christian's love different?

    *Our love flows from Christ's work on the cross, which gives us the ability to love sacrificially without desire for return (v. 5:2; see also Eph. 2:10)*

8. What is the significance of "abiding" in verses 15 and 16?

    15 *It is a natural outflow of our confession of faith*

    16 *We come to know and believe God's love*

9. Look up John 15:4–15. In that passage, what are the positive and negative consequences of either abiding or not abiding?

| Positive consequences | Negative consequences |
| --- | --- |
| Bear fruit (vv. 4, 5, 16) | Nothing (v. 5) |
| Ask whatever (vv. 7, 16) | Thrown away (v. 6) |
| Your requests will be done for you (vv. 7, 16) | Withered (v. 6) |
| You will dwell in Christ's love forever (vv. 9, 10) | Burned (v. 6) |

## For Additional Study

We rightly feel the burden of our loved ones' problems and are eager to help. However, often our desires turn in on themselves. We feel as though *we* are the ones responsible for fixing their problems and saving them from suffering or rescuing them from sin. This kind of "Savior complex" is a trap; it's the opposite of Christ's calling.

List what Christ has done for us from Isaiah 53:2–12. Make note of the ways in which this demonstrates how impossible it is for you to try to do the work of the Savior.

| Verse | Christ's calling | Struggle |
|---|---|---|
| 2 | No earthly dignity | (Answers will vary) |
| 3 | Despised | |
| 3 | Rejected | |
| 3 | Acquainted with grief | |
| 3 | Despised | |
| 3 | Disrespected | |
| 4 | Bore OUR grief | |
| 4 | Carried OUR sorrow | |
| 4 | Afflicted by God | |
| 5 | Took OUR sins | |
| 5 | Pierced for US | |
| 5 | He was chastised | |
| 5 | He was wounded | |
| 6 | Willingly took our iniquity | |
| 7 | Oppressed | |
| 7 | Afflicted | |
| 7 | Silence | |
| | | Continued . . . |

| Verse | Christ's calling | Struggle |
|:---:|---|---|
| 8 | Taken away unjustly | |
| 8 | Cut off from the land of the living | |
| 8 | Stricken for US | |
| 9 | Buried with the wicked | |
| 9 | Buried for nothing he did | |
| 10 | Crushed—by the will of God | |
| 10 | Grieved | |
| 10 | A satisfactory offering | |
| 11 | His death = Our life | |
| 12 | Numbered with transgressors | |

# Knowing One Another

## Digging into the Word

1. Proverbs is full of passages that teach us about the importance of listening well. Summarize the main point of each of the following proverbs and then make a list of what you learn about patient listening from them.

### Proverbs 10:19
- Many words are ripe with the potential for sin
- Not everything that is said needs to be said

### Proverbs 12:18
- Using fewer words is wise
- Rash words cause pain
- Carefully considering what is said blesses those who hear
- Wise words heal

### Proverbs 15:28
- There is a way to speak righteously as well as a way to speak wickedly
- Righteous people think before they speak

### Proverbs 17:27
- Disciplining our speech is important for communication
- Using fewer words make the speaker look knowledgeable
- Knowledge should inform our speech

### Proverbs 18:13
- Listening is an important communication skill
- Listen well, ask questions, hear people.

### Proverbs 18:17
- Those who wait to speak until they have all the right information are wise
- Knowledge is desirable for intelligence and wisdom
- Hearing both sides to a story is helpful

## Proverbs 20:5

- ○ People who stay calm are empathetic.
- ○ People don't always express themselves well; however, how we communicate can be helpful to another's well-being.
- ○ Good questions draw out the heart.

2. How would applying the truth of this proverb help you to listen, ask questions, or know others better?

> *If one gives an answer before he hears, it is his folly and shame. (Proverbs 18:13).*

(Answers vary)

3. Which of these proverbs do you need to remember the most? Memorize it!

(Answers vary)

4. Where else in Scripture might expand on the truth mentioned in this proverb?

> *The heart of the righteous ponders how to answer but the mouth of the wicked pours out evil things. (Proverbs. 15:28).*

> *"Know this, my beloved brothers: let every person be quick to hear, slow to speak, slow to anger; for the anger of man does not produce the righteousness of God" (James 1:19–20).*

5. How might the relationships you're in now be impacted if you applied the truth of this proverb?

> *The purpose in a man's heart is like deep water, but a man of understanding will draw it out. (Proverbs 20:5).*

(Answers vary)

## SERVING ONE ANOTHER

### DIGGING INTO THE WORD

1.  Read John 13:1–17

2.  Describe the significance of "his hour."

    *It was Christ's final time with his disciples.*

3.  Describe the act of servanthood that Christ engaged in at this supper (vv. 4–12)

    *Set aside his own physical needs (the meal)*

    *Humbled himself (removed his own clothing)*

    *Took the role of a servant (girl, actually)*

    *Addressed his disciple's most pressing, physical need*

4.  In this pivotal moment in his ministry, did Jesus choose to show his love primarily through words or actions?

    *Actions*

5.  What does this act say about the type of caregiving we should be giving as Christ's servants? (v. 14)

    *Body and soul*

6.  Jesus's kingdom is an upside-down kingdom. Contrast the world's pattern of approaching messy people with Christ's.

| World | Christ |
|---|---|
| Boundaries | *Wash one another's feet (vv. 5, 12, 14) i.e., intimacy* |
| Formal setting | *During supper (v. 2) i.e., anywhere* |
| Appointments | *Rose from supper (v. 4) i.e., inopportune times* |
| Limited involvement | *"loved them to the end" (v.1) i.e., never done loving* |

## For Additional Study

John tells us that Jesus is the Word. "In the beginning was the Word, and the Word was with God, and the Word was God." Look up the following passages and describe some of the things the Word *does*, noting the practical significance of the act for the recipient.

| Verse | What the Word Does | Practical Significance |
|---|---|---|
| John 2:1–11 | Changed water into wine | Honored the guests of the wedding, made the host look generous |
| Luke 5:1–11 | Brought in a large number of fish | Rewarded the fishermen's hard work |
| Mark 1:30–31 | Healed Simon's mother-in-law | Gave her an opportunity to give back in service to Christ |
| Mark 1:40–45 | Healed a leper | Provided the man with a mission (spread the news) |
| Matt. 8:5–13 | Healed the centurion's servant | Relieved his physical suffering |
| Luke 7:11–18 | Raised the widow's son from the dead | Provided for her physical needs and safety |
| Matt. 8:23–27 | Stilled a storm | Alleviated the disciples' fears |
| Matt. 8:28–34 | Healed the two demon-possessed men | Provided access for those who would need to pass through the region |
| Luke 8:43–48 | Cured the bleeding woman | Gave her peace—opened up an entire world of possibilities for her well-being and happiness (i.e., possible marriage and/or children and the accompanying safety each provided) |

Continued . . .

| Verse | What the Word Does | Practical Significance |
|---|---|---|
| Matt. 14:15–21 | Fed the five thousand | Satisfied their hunger without inconveniencing them |
| John 11:1–46 | Raised Lazarus | Comforted his sisters, revived Lazarus! |
| John 21:25 | More than can be written | We, as the recipients of all that Christ did, are eternally blessed |

## SPEAKING TO ONE ANOTHER

### DIGGING INTO THE WORD

1. Read Hebrews 3:12–15

2. What is the main characteristic of an evil heart in verse 12?

   *Unbelief*

2a. How should this shape your loving confrontation toward those living in a mess?

   *Help them believe in the God of the Bible! "The low view of God entertained almost universally among Christians is the cause of a hundred lesser evils everywhere among us." (A.W. Tozer, The Knowledge of the Holy)*

3. What does biblical exhortation entail? (v. 13) (See also Heb. 10:24–25; 1 Thess. 5:14)

   *Stir up one another to good works and love*

   *Encourage all to remain in community with the family of God*

   *Encourage one another*

   *Admonish the unruly*

   *Encourage the fainthearted*

   *Help the weak*

   *Be patient with all men*

4. What does it mean to "share in Christ?"

   *Steadfast confidence in faith until the end*

4a. Write down some of the ways you've been encouraged (through God's Word) to have confidence in God.

   (Answers vary)

5. In between seeking God in prayer and waiting to hear God's answer (Ps. 5:3; Heb. 3:15), what should people stuck in a mess do so that their hearts will not harden? How can you help them? (Heb. 3:12)

   *Take care*

   *Engage in caregiving*

   *"Caring = Speaking" Scott Mehl*

## For Additional Study

1. In the general session Scott quoted Wayne Mack saying, "Hope is a biblically based expectation of good." Therefore, hope indicates that:

   o God is real (*Rom. 1:20; John 10:22–33*)

   o Transformation is possible (*Acts 9:1–19; Acts 18:8*)

   o The best is yet to come (*Rev. 21:4; Col. 3:1–4*)

2. What passages in the Bible substantiate these characteristics of hope?

# GOSPELING ONE ANOTHER (PART 1)

## DIGGING INTO THE WORD

1. Read 1 Corinthians 15:1–5

2. Identify what Paul says is,

2a. Our problem

*We are sinners (v. 3)*

2b. God's solution

*Christ died, was buried, raised from the dead, and his resurrection was witnessed (vv. 3–5)*

2c. Our response

*Stand, hold fast, believe (vv. 1, 2)*

3. How does the gospel continue to progressively work in these passages?

*The gospel continues to save (v. 2)*

4. What's the significance of "in accordance with the Scriptures"?

*God has set the standard by which all people must comply; God IS the standard.*

## FOR ADDITIONAL STUDY

1. On a sheet of paper, create two columns. On one side, explain how you would share the gospel with someone who is struggling under the weight of sin. On the other side, explain how you would provide hope through the gospel for someone who is struggling under the weight of suffering.

1a. What is the same? Where are the differences in emphasis?

*(Answers vary)*

## GOSPELING ONE ANOTHER (PART 2)

### DIGGING INTO THE WORD

1. Read Psalm 111.

2. Write down what these passages tell us about God.

| | |
|---|---|
| 111:2 | *His works are great* |
| 111:3 | *His works are full of splendor and majesty* |
| 111:3 | *His righteousness endures forever* |
| 111:4 | *His works are memorable* |
| 111:4 | *He is gracious and merciful* |
| 111:5 | *He provides* |
| 111:5 | *He remembers his covenant forever* |
| 111:6 | *His works are powerful* |
| 111:6 | *He gives his inheritance to his people* |
| 111:7 | *His works are faithful and just* |
| 111:7 | *His precepts are trustworthy* |
| 111:8 | *His precepts are established forever* |
| 111:8 | *His precepts are performed with faithfulness and uprightness* |
| 111:9 | *He redeems* |
| 111:9 | *He commanded his covenant forever* |
| 111:9 | *His name is holy and awesome* |
| 111:10 | *His praise endures forever* |

# Appendices

# EPHESIANS 1-3 BLESSINGS

BLESSINGS THAT EQUIP THE SAINTS FOR THE WORK OF MINISTRY

| Verse | Blessing |
| --- | --- |
| 1:3 | Every spiritual blessing in the heavenly places |
| 1:4 | He chose us |
| 1:4 | He made us holy and blameless before him |
| 1:5 | He predestined us (also Eph. 1:11) |
| 1:5 | He adopted us |
| 1:6 | Blessed us in the beloved |
| 1:7 | Redemption (in him) |
| 1:7 | Forgiveness for our trespasses |
| 1:7 | Riches of his grace |
| 1:8 | Lavished us |
| 1:9 | Made known the mystery of his will |
| 1:10 | United us |
| 1:11 | Gave us an inheritance |
| 1:12 | Made us the praise of his glory |
| 1:13 | Sealed us with the promised Holy Spirit |

*Continued . . .*

| Verse | Blessing |
|---|---|
| 1:14 | Guaranteed our inheritance |
| 1:17 | Gives a spirit of wisdom |
| 1:17 | Gives revelation of the knowledge of him |
| 1:18 | Enlightens our eyes |
| 1:18 | Know the hope to which we are called |
| 1:18 | Know the riches of his glorious inheritance |
| 1:19 | Know immeasurable greatness of his power toward us |
| 1:20 | God worked in Christ for us, raised him from the dead, seated him at his right hand |
| 1:22 | Put all things under Christ's feet |
| 1:22 | Gave Christ as the head of the church |
| 2:4 | Rich in mercy toward us |
| 2:4 | Loved us |
| 2:5 | Made us alive together in Christ |
| 2:5 | Saved us by grace |
| 2:6 | Raised us up with Christ |
| 2:6 | Seated us in the heavenly places in Christ |
| 2:8 | Salvation (the gift from God) |
| 2:10 | Ability to do good works |
| 2:12 | United to Christ |
| 2:12 | Joined with Israel |
| 2:12 | Familiar with the covenants of promise |
| 2:12 | Have hope |
| 2:12 | With God in this world |
| 2:13 | Brought near |
| 2:14 | Peace |
| 2:14 | One with God |
| 2:14 | Broken down dividing wall of hostility |

*Continued . . .*

| Verse | Blessing |
|-------|----------|
| 2:15 | Abolished the law of commandments |
| 2:15 | Created one new man in himself |
| 2:15 | Made peace |
| 2:16 | Reconciled us with God |
| 2:16 | Killed hostility |
| 2:17 | Sent his Son |
| 2:17 | Preached peace |
| 2:18 | Gave access to him |
| 2:19 | Gave citizenship |
| 2:19 | Became family |
| 2:22 | Became a dwelling place for God |
| 3:5 | Revealed mystery |
| 3:6 | Became fellow heirs |
| 3:6 | Became members of one body |
| 3:6 | Became partakers of the promise |
| 3:8 | Recipients of the grace given to Paul to preach |
| 3:10 | Manifold wisdom of God made known to us |
| 3:11 | Eternal purposes of Christ realized |
| 3:12 | Boldness |
| 3:12 | Confidence |
| 4:1 | Called |
| 4:1 | Ability to walk worthy |
| 4:2 | Humility |
| 4:2 | Gentleness |
| 4:2 | Patience |
| 4:2 | Ability to bear with one another in love |
| 4:3 | Unity |
| 4:3 | Bond of peace |

*Continued . . .*

| Verse | Blessing |
|-------|----------|
| 4:4 | One body |
| 4:4 | One Spirit |
| 4:4 | One hope |
| 4:5 | One Lord |
| 4:5 | One faith |
| 4:5 | One baptism |
| 4:6 | One God |
| 4:6 | One Father |
| 4:6 | Authority |
| 4:7 | Grace (according to Christ's gift) |
| 4:8 | Gifts |
| 4:11 | Apostles |
| 4:11 | Prophets |
| 4:11 | Evangelists |
| 4:11 | Shepherds |
| 4:11 | Teachers |
| 4:13 | Unity |
| 4:13 | Knowledge of the Son |
| 4:13 | Maturity |
| 4:13 | Stature of the fullness Christ |
| 4:14 | Maturity |
| 4:15 | Maturity |
| 4:16 | Unity, growth, love |

# PSALM 68 BLESSINGS

## BLESSINGS GOD GIVES HIS PEOPLE

| Verse | Blessing |
|---|---|
| 1 | Our enemies are scattered |
| 1 | Haters flee |
| 2 | The wicked perish |
| 3 | The righteous have gladness |
| 3 | The righteous exult before God |
| 3 | The righteous are jubilant with joy |
| 4 | We are able to sing praises |
| 4 | We are able to lift a song |
| 4 | We are privileged to exult the Lord |
| 5 | God is our Father! |
| 5 | Our Lord is our protector |
| 6 | He gives us a home |
| 6 | He gives prosperity |
| 6 | The rebellious are sent away from him and us |
| 7 | He is our guide in the wilderness |
| 8 | He has subdued the earth |
| 8 | He has given rain (i.e., made provision) |
| 9 | He restored our inheritance |

*Continued . . .*

| Verse | Blessing |
|---|---|
| 10 | He provides a dwelling for his flock |
| 10 | He gives provision for the needy |
| 11 | He gives us his Word |
| 12 | Kings and armies flee |
| 12 | He gives *us* the spoil |
| 14 | He scatters kings |
| 16 | He makes himself a dwelling place |
| 17 | He gives power |
| 17 | The Lord dwelling in his sanctuary |
| 18 | The Lord ascending |
| 18 | The Lord leading captives away |
| 18 | The Lord receiving the spoil |
| 18 | The Lord making his dwelling place |
| 19 | The Lord bears us up |
| 19 | The Lord is our salvation |
| 20 | He gives deliverance from death |
| 21 | He will strike our enemies |
| 22 | He will bring us back |
| 23 | He gives us a portion |
| 28 | God's power is worked out *for us* |
| 30 | Even the beasts are rebuked |
| 30 | Those who lust after tribute are trampled underfoot |
| 30 | Those who delight in war are scattered |
| 33 | He gives us his voice |
| 34 | He provides us with the ability to ascribe power to God |
| 35 | He gives power |
| 35 | He gives strength |

# ENDNOTES

1. While the *Intro to (Messy) Care and Discipleship* is designed to be used in a small group, individuals can also work their way through the program on their own.
2. The structure for this section is adapted from Greg Gilbert, What is the Gospel? (Wheaton, IL: Crossway, 2010), 31–33.
3. A.W. Tozer, The Knowledge of the Holy (New York, NY: HarperCollins, 1961), 2.

# COUNSEL
## FOR THE
# HEART

### A RESOURCE for WORD-BASED
### TRANSFORMATION and
### PRACTICAL DISCIPLESHIP

# Loving Messy People:
## The Messy Art of Helping One Another Become More Like Jesus

*Scott Mehl*

Trade Paperback, 224pp
ISBN: 978-1-63342-183-7

*Anxiety... Depression... Lust... Addiction... Trauma... Chronic illness... Unfulfilling work... Ungrateful children... Unpredictable circumstances... Eating problems... Relational problems... Financial problems... Pain... Suffering... Sin...*

*Life's a mess.* And nobody escapes it. Your life's a mess. Your friends and family's lives are a mess too.

Thankfully God has a plan to deal with the mess. It involves you, and it involves me. Even with all of our messes, God wants to use every one of us in the lives of those around us to be part of his glorious rescue plan in their lives.

But, if you don't know exactly what to do or even where to start, *Loving Messy People* is for you. This book is a practical handbook designed to equip you for each of the messy situations in your life and the lives of those around you. Filled with real-life stories, biblical truth, and practical wisdom, Loving Messy People will show you how God wants to use you in his plan to transform the mess in people's lives into something redemptive and beautiful.

"*If you want to help messy people, or if you are one, then this book is for you.*"
—Elyse M. Fitzpatrick (Author of *Counsel from the Cross*)

"*Loving Messy People is a biblical treasure chest of encouragement, hope, pastoral wisdom, and practical instruction*"
—Ryan Townsend (Executive Director, 9Marks)

"*Mehl ... shows the reader how to use biblical principles to care for people in very realistic (and messy) life situations.*"
—Jim Newheiser (Associate Professor of Pastoral Theology and the Director of the Christian Counseling Program, Reformed Theological Seminary, Charlotte)

"*If you're like me and need help with your messy life, or you just want to help others to take simple steps forward out of chaos, buy and give away Loving Messy People.*"
—Dave Harvey (President of Great Commission Collective; Founder of AmICalled.com; Author of *When Sinners Say I Do, Rescuing Ambition,* and *I Still Do*)

"*... real stories, pastoral wisdom, and piercing application of the gospel...*"
—J.A. Medders (Pastor of Preaching and Theology, Redeemer Church; Author of *Humble Calvinism*)

## About Shepherd Press Publications

- They are gospel driven.
- They are heart focused.
- They are life changing.

## Our Invitation to You

We passionately believe that what we are publishing can be of benefit to you, your family, your friends, and your work colleagues. So we are inviting you to join our online mailing list so that we may reach out to you with news about our latest and forthcoming publications, and with special offers.
Visit:

**www.shepherdpress.com/newsletter**

and provide your name and email address.